Grace

and

Grief

*A Widow's Journey
with Family and
Friends*

Paula McVay

ISBN 978-1-68570-797-2 (paperback)
ISBN 978-1-68570-798-9 (digital)

Christian Faith Publishing
832 Park Avenue
Meadville, PA 16335
www.christianfaithpublishing.com

Printed in the United States of America

Blurbs

It's real. It's practical. It's hopeful. Paula writes with eye opening candor, telling the story of her ongoing journey through grief. Whatever the loss, these pages provide navigational beacons to get the reader through to peaceful waters.

—Carlton Harvey, PhD, Former District Superintendent, Pastor

Paula McVay doesn't sugarcoat her journey through grief. Her pain, loss, anxiety, and confusion are openly shared. Her firm belief that God loves her allows her to be honest with God and look to Him for healing. From this experience, she gives valuable and practical guidance on how to survive and then thrive after losing a spouse.

—David Schriemer MD, Family Physician

As a grief counselor and therapist, I was happy to read Paula McVay's hopeful and encouraging book on grief. Having worked with Hospice for over twenty years, I know how helpful it can be for bereaved people to know they are not traveling this road alone. Paula uses her own and other stories to explore this universal as well as personal and individual journey. With liberal use of comforting scriptures, as well as many helpful suggestions for coping at the end of each chapter, and a nice resource list, this is a book that one can turn to again and again on their journeys of grief.

—Barbara L. Morris, LMSW, Grief Counselor and Therapist

Paula is transparently honest, vulnerable, raggedly real, straightforward, helpful, courageous, and empathetic. Her book shows us ways to face our grief and for family and friends to know how to help. She gives insight by embracing the Lord while doing hard work emotionally. Her helpful everyday suggestions are inspirational and doable. We, too, can go from our nightmarish loneliness to a sacred embrace of God's love and then on to inner peace. The greatest concept is that of sharing our grief with a friend! This book is a valuable tool for me, both personally and as a counselor.

—Charles Pickens, MA, Pastor and Chaplain

Contents

Acknowledgments

I am "overflowing with thankfulness" for

- My three adult sons and five grandsons who have traveled on this journey with me through many tears, great memories, laughs, and encouragement. My special thanks to my daughter-in-law, Lori, who has published a book on leadership in conjunction with earning her PhD. She has listened and encouraged nearly every week during our family dinner times. My youngest son has helped me with any technology needs...always patient and willing to listen.

- The widows who were willing to be interviewed and to patiently listen as I read parts of the book to them. We comforted each other and made connections each time we talked.

- A longtime friend, fellow widow, and pastor's wife who is my closest prayer partner. In her quiet and loving way, she would often ask me how I was progressing. Eventually, she began to gently nudge me to reach deadlines.

- My neighborhood walking partner, a fellow widow, and a nurse who listened on our two-and-three-mile walks. Her insight brought a whole new perspective.

- My lifelong couple friends who have not only prayed for me but have included me in dinners, vacations, and praying for our children.

- Ladies in my Bible study and prayer group who faithfully prayed and encouraged me.

- My church family who weekly extends their love and even makes sure I get plenty of hugs.

- Most of all, I am thankful for the direction and impressions of my closest friend and companion, Jesus. So many times, I would have to stop writing because I was so overwhelmed with grief and no words would come. My simple plea for help resulted in words flowing from my mind to my fingers. Amazement enveloped me as I began to praise God. "So then, just as you received Christ Jesus as Lord, continue to live in Him, rooted and built up in Him, strengthened in the faith as you were taught and overflowing with thankfulness" (Colossians 2:6–7).

Introduction

Wow! I've been writing this book for seven years. I thought I would never finish. On a recent broadcast by Dr. David Jeremiah, senior pastor of Shadow Mountain Community Church in San Diego, California, explained that if an idea comes into your head that seems easy, it probably isn't from God because He often asks us to do things that seem almost impossible. Yes, I do like to write and have had several articles published in a Christian women's magazine, but those were just short stories. I've tried to quit writing this book several times. When telling the stories of mine and other widows' grief, my emotions were all over the place as memories washed over me. I did set up a notebook with my titles and added clips as thoughts bombarded my mind. Quitting was not an option. I just kept feeling that nudge from the Holy Spirit to "keep at it." Friends and other widows were always asking me if I was finished. Even my doctor and financial advisor asked for a copy.

Perhaps one of the reasons it has taken me so long to complete the book might be that I have more "inspiration" than "perspiration." God's timing is always perfect, though. In the past few years, things have happened that I needed to include such as facing more challenges from simple plumbing issues to dealing with a prodigal son. Had I written in the first years, I would not have been able to share the struggles and strengths of the more than twenty other widows whom I have interviewed. Many of the thirty plus books that I have read about grief were written in the first few years of the widow's grief journey. Of course they were helpful, but I have been through more years, valleys, and mountain to realize that God's grace remains through all the years. We can think we are doing so well. I remember telling my pastor son after the first year, "I've really turned a corner.

I think I can make it." "No more crying spells or deep feelings of sadness." Then…just watching a Hallmark movie would bring it all back. During the second year of my friend Mary's grief, she called and asked, "Why didn't you tell me the second year was rougher than the first? Truly, I was hoping her second year would be better. As expressed by Dr. Robert G. Robinson, MD, professor emeritus of geriatric psychiatry at the University of Iowa, "Grief, rather than being a linear progression of stages, is more like a roller coaster of emotions."

The years have also taught me how little I knew about the grieving process. As a pastor's wife, I often tried to comfort those in grief and I'm sure my sentiments were appreciated. After all, I had read books and studied psychology; however, I had not experienced deep personal grief. Now, I can offer help to comforters by including ways to help and things to say and maybe "not to say." Family members and friends will begin to realize the importance of just being there, not only in the first year, but throughout the years. Adult children of older widows will begin to realize how much their mom really needs them. Most widows whom I have interviewed try not to show their pain. Their friends and family are likely to think they have moved on; however, the widow never quits thinking about her soul mate… especially on those special days like anniversaries and holidays. One thing I've learned from talking with other widows is that Doug and I had an uncommonly deep friendship and spiritual bonding. Expressed beautifully by a widow who served in a leadership role with her husband on our district were these words. "Paula, you and I were married to extraordinary men: therefore our grief is not an ordinary grief."

As I have read and studied numerous books on grief and grace, I've noticed that many of the writers are doctors, counselors, lawyers, or celebrities. My credentials of a masters' degree in education, thirty years of teaching both elementary, secondary and college, and being a pastor's wife and mom dim, in comparison; however, I speak from the heart and know that I am thankful for God's continual prodding and for the encouragement of friends and family. As a teacher and children's worship director, I've used my story telling skills to reel in readers as they sense a new hope rising from deep within. Of course every person has a different story, but we have many things in common. My particular story is one of two people from dysfunctional families, meeting at a Christian college, being so thankful for God's intervention in our lives, and loving each other so much that we were almost inseparable. Even though God wonderfully saved us both in our teens, we had to go back into those homes to deal with pressing issues.

My first impression for a title for this book was *Wonder Widow*, not as in Wonder Woman, but as in "I wonder how I can do this." My "wondering" has turned to knowing the wonder of God's grace. My desire is that readers will find comfort in knowing they are not alone as they make connections to other who are grieving. May they find this book realistic, but humorous, helpful, and practical. Friends and relatives of those who are grieving will also gain wisdom for helping grievers. Married people of all ages will perceive how God's grace will strengthen their marriage throughout their own journeys. Even though I don't have my godly spouse, Isaiah 54:5 tells me God is my husband. I know He will continue to be faithful as I call out to him daily, sometimes more desperately than others. "In the morning, O Lord, you hear my voice, in the morning I lay my requests before you and wait in expectation" (Ps. 5:3 NIV).

My life verse has always been, "My grace is sufficient for you, for my power is made perfect in weakness" (2 Cor. 12:9 NIV). I was weak in dealing with my abusive family, but God made me strong and gave me wisdom to handle life, be a strong Christian leader of the fifty youth in my church and leader in school organizations. I didn't have the skills to do this. No one in my home ever taught me or gave me the support, but my church family stepped in and gave me that confidence, love, and encouragement. I had no ideas how to make college happen. No one in my family had ever graduated from college or graduate school. I surely had to depend on God as I began my teaching career since I had prepared to teach lower elementary and was placed in an eighth grade English and writing class. God knew I would need that. I wasn't sure that I would ever finish this book, but I have truly found His grace showing up over and over again throughout this journey. Please join me.

1

Caring for Your Loved One during Their Last Days

Celebrating my retirement from thirty years of teaching sent us dancing up the lighted, winding staircase of the mammoth ship on our first cruise. As we strolled along on the top deck, hand in hand, discussing all the fun shows we would enjoy and the gorgeous beach stops, Doug squeezed my hand and said, "I need to go back to the cabin for a while. I must have a little flu bug." Within an hour, his fever had climbed to 104 degrees with oozing sores erupting all over his body. A nurse from the infirmary immediately dispatched a wheelchair to transport him down to the lower level infirmary. All Doug could think about was how the people were staring at him and probably thought he had a contagious disease. God provided us with this amazing and compassionate Russian doctor who put his hand on my shoulder as he looked down from his six-foot-five stature to my five-foot-four. He tried to assure me that Doug would be all right and that his vitals remained stable. The Argentine nurse administered a powerful antibiotic and sent us back to our cabin with instructions to return the next morning.

Morning did not come soon enough. About 3:00 a.m., I had to call for the Filipino nurse to come for Doug because the fever had not broken and the sores had begun to bleed. Everyone on staff was from a different country and treated us with great dignity and compassion…a truly multicultural experience. The fever finally broke early that morning so Doug was escorted back to our cabin in a wheelchair, again feeling as if everyone in the elevator was staring. I was instructed to transport him back to the infirmary every few hours for intravenous antibiotic. Although he was in excruciating pain for the hour-long process, he never complained.

As I was able to return to our cabin while Doug was being treated, anxiety crept over me like a spiderweb. I felt totally alone and isolated since my cell phone was not working, leaving no way to contact my family or friends. As the balance on my debit card was quickly vanishing, I cried out to the Lord to calm me. Right there in that little cabin, I felt impressed to read Psalm 77. As I read aloud, a peace seemed to sweep over me from the top of my head to the tip of my feet. Verse 13 affirms, "Your ways, Oh God, are holy. What God is as great as our God? You are the God who performs miracles" (NIV).

Suddenly, the cabin phone rang. My youngest son was calling from New York where he worked for a large accounting firm. What a miracle for this to happen just as I was preparing to return to the infirmary! When I told him about his dad, he insisted, "Get him off at the next island, and I will fly there to help you." I was so calm and full of the Lord's presence (truly a miracle) that I told him I felt it was best to keep his dad on the ship because of the good doctors and nurses. I was also able to share my experience of reading the Psalm aloud. My son is a wonderfully sweet and caring young man; however, he had made life choices so different from his family upbringing. Had he called a few moments sooner, I would not have had the amazing grace of Jesus to share with him. I'm sure the whole event was a part of the process in my son's spiritual growth as well as in mine.

"You need to see an immunologist when you return to the States," the compassionate Russian doctor expressed in his heavy accent. I had never heard of such but assured him I would put it at the top of my "to do" list. Doug did get a little better as we finished the cruise. He would sit on one of the decks and encourage me to take part in the line dancing and other activities. Later, at home, he made people laugh as he told them about his being extremely ill while his wife was up on the deck dancing and singing. (So not true.) That sense of humor and God's strength and grace carried us through five more years.

Since Doug did have an autoimmune disease, he was told to stay away from people as much as possible. We were careful, but Doug refused to quit doing the things he loved: preaching and teaching. He worked for an organization that helped churches go through transition. We would move to a temporary home in another city, and Doug, in his gentle compassionate way, would lead the church "out of anxiety into anticipation." What a joy to watch God use Doug's loving leadership skills as the people responded so positively!

Each year or assignment seemed to bring at least one frightful episode of illness with Doug's having a high fever and a cough. After a short hospital stay, he would bounce back and be on the job. I began to wonder how many times this could happen since he would seem to be on the verge of dying one day and up working the next. One such episode took place in a church in our neighboring state of Indiana. With his compromised immunity, Doug contracted type B influenza and pneumonia. Specialists were called in and did not give us a lot of hope. With a huge snowstorm in progress, a group of twenty-eight people from the church in which we were serving, gathered in the hospital lobby, held hands, and prayed for God's healing touch. This group included a godly physician who eventually helped diagnose Doug's disease. Two days later Doug was released from the hospital and the next Monday he was back in the office. I did not know how long Doug would live but knew that God was in control and I would trust him. I leaned on God's word from (Col. 1:17, NIV). "He is before all things and in Him, all things hold together." We had three more years of beautiful ministry in two more churches.

For our next ministry assignment, we were all settled into the spacious parsonage on a beautiful wooded lot just five minutes from the beach on Lake Michigan. Doug was doing well when suddenly, he began coughing and his fever shot up to 103 degrees. I wondered if this would be the time God would allow him to go home to heaven. Panic creeped up within me as I lay on the couch in the living room with these thoughts racing through my mind. "I barely know where we are in this city, much less where the hospital is. I don't know whom to call." God answered me in that still small voice. "Trust me." I opened my Bible to Psalm 77...yes, the same one I had read on the cruise ship. I reread verse 13, "O God, your ways are holy. Is there any god as mighty as you? You are the God of miracles and wonders." That same peace that had come upon me on the cruise ship washed over me. I went back to the bedroom where Doug was no longer coughing and his temperature had returned to normal. I jumped all around on the king-sized bed the church had provided for us shouting, "God has touched you. Praise His holy name." A few hours later, Doug was in the pulpit delivering another masterful sermon.

Once again, it was not God's appointed time. "There is a time for everything, and a season for every activity under Heaven" (Eccles. 3:1) In my humanness, I once again wondered how many times this would happen and when God would call Doug home. We actually began to talk about when that time might be. Some would say that we should have had more faith and never have discussed the future that way; however, we felt God's comfort and companionship and knew we were ready for His plan...whatever it might be. A few months later, we had to leave that beautiful place by the beach because Doug was diagnosed with leukemia and needed to be closer to his doctors in our hometown to undergo chemotherapy. Once again, we realized that God's ways are higher than ours as the prophet Isaiah recorded in Isaiah 55:8–9. "For my thoughts are not your thoughts, neither are your ways my ways, declares the Lord. As the heavens are higher than the earth, so are my ways higher than your ways and my thoughts than your thoughts."

Even then, we treasured each day and began to realize even more that God was with us. In our little condo back home that looks out over a luscious forest area, we sat on the couch talking about what heaven might be like. We loved learning scripture verses together. One of our favorite was from 2 Corinthians 4:16–17,

> Therefore we do not lose heart (hope)
> though outwardly we are wasting away, inwardly,

we are being renewed day by day. For our light
and momentary troubles are achieving for us an
eternal glory that far outweighs them all. So we
fix our eyes (focus) not on what is seen, but what
is unseen. For what is seen is temporary and what
is unseen is eternal.

We would cry and rejoice at God's grace and comfort. Doug
would often ask me to play a hymn on the piano as we sang. He
shared his favorite ones and his favorite scripture passages. We would
pray for each of our three adult sons and their families and rejoice
over our new grandson born in September before Doug passed in
February.

Even during these last few months, God provided for us financially. The organization for which Doug was employed asked him
to mentor the new pastor. They paid us enough to help meet all our
obligations. Doug had all our finances set up on the computer and
patiently explained how to do everything. We kept saying, "Just in
case the need should arise" because Doug was still quite articulate
and pretty energetic on most days.

I do remember one day when he could not stop coughing. I
asked if he felt the need to call an ambulance. He looked at me with
those piercing big blue eyes and asked, "Do you think I'm going to
die?"

Sadly, I responded with "Do you feel that way?"

He replied, "I'm not going to die any time soon, but I'm ready
whenever the Lord calls. I just want to make sure you are ready and
will be okay." I assured him that I knew God's grace would be sufficient to take care of me and for him to just concentrate on getting well. He died two months later; however, in the meantime, he
preached a great sermon at one of our former churches on December
31 and passed away on February 17 after a ten-day hospital stay.
Those from that congregation who came to the funeral kept saying
how healthy he had looked just a few weeks prior.

Our cancer doctor suggested that Doug skip his fourth chemo
treatment since he was doing so well. The next week, we went for

the usual bloodwork when just as we were about to leave the doctor's office, immobilizing pain struck. We called the doctor back into our room and asked if he could prescribe something for pain. He said we would have to go to the hospital for more tests, which usually meant twelve to sixteen hours in the emergency room. Thankfully, the nurse there did give him some pain medicine, and after eight more hours, Doug was diagnosed with pancreatitis and hospitalized for ten days. I am thankful for this doctor. Even though I felt he was not being compassionate at the time, I now realize that he knew Doug's time was close, and he wanted him to be in the hospital where he would receive continual care. Once again, God was working for the good in a seemingly hopeless situation. Romans 8:28 tells us, "And we know that in all things, God works for the good of those who love Him." It doesn't say all things are good and all prayers for healing will be answered the way we desire. It just lets us know God is in control and His grace is sufficient.

During those ten days in the hospital, friends brought in food, coffee, and gifts. Our wonderful family doctor visited one afternoon for two hours on his "day off." What a comfort he was to our three adult sons as he prayed for our family and for Doug's healing. Even the hospital staff seemed to love to be in the room to just chat. Perhaps they sensed the presence of God. I began to wonder what I would do if he died in the hospital. My faith for healing was strong; however, reality was staring me in the face. I made a list of the people with their phone numbers that I would contact: the pastor who would conduct the service, the funeral home, life insurance, Social Security office, places with scheduled appointments, friends, and family.

I kept thinking Doug would bounce back; however, on the seventh day, he became weaker. He wanted all of his four grandsons to be present. As my daughter-in-law sat the baby on the rails with his legs dangling over, his papa took great delight in tickling him and hearing his giggles. The four-year-old wanted Papa to get out of bed so they could "play cars." The ten- and twelve-year-olds understood more about what was happening since they had lost their biological mom to cancer just a few years earlier. On the ninth evening, when everyone was getting ready to leave, my sons were deciding who would spend the night. I had been there for the past four so mentioned that I should probably go home for some rest. Doug looked at all of them and said in his clear, rich voice, "Paula, I want you to stay." I think he knew then that his time was soon.

About 3:00 a.m., I asked Doug if he wanted some pain medication. He assured me that he wanted to stay alert, but he did agree to take something to relax. I crawled up on to the bed with him. He lifted his hands and began to rub my back and tell me how much he loved me and that I was the best sweetheart, wife, and mom to our boys he could ever have wished for. This was especially amazing because he had not been able to lift his hands for the last few hours. I knew he was saying goodbye. I sat back in the chair beside him and saw him lift his hand toward heaven and exclaim, "Look, Paula. There's a big banquet room up there. Do you think there will be room for us?"

Through my tears, I said, "Oh yes, you must be getting a glimpse of heaven, but let's don't go just yet."

His last words were from Psalm 3:3: "But You are a shield around me, Oh Lord. You bestow glory on me and lift up my head." He would intersperse his own words of "Thank you, Jesus. Thank you for your glory. Thank you for your grace. Oh, thank you for lifting up my head. I'm ready, Lord. Take me into your glory." Some might ask, "Why didn't God heal him this time?" I know God can and does heal, but I do not know how or when. I know too that I can talk with Him anytime and He gives me comfort. That is the true gift of healing.

Once again, I experienced that overwhelming peace as I was able to sleep in the recliner by his bed. At 5:10 a.m., my son woke me to say, "Mom, Dad is passing now." When I asked how he knew, he instructed me to listen for his breathing as it became slower and slower. My son had been with his first wife as she passed away a few years before. Even now, as I write this experience, I pray that same verse from Psalm 3:3. "Oh Lord, thank you for being a shield around me as I remember and write. Thank you for bestowing glory and continuing to lift up my head."

I couldn't believe how gracefully Doug slipped away...no struggle, only a sweet, sweet peace. As I rubbed his arm, his body immediately turned cold. Even in this sad moment, I smiled as I looked at the clock and told my son, "Look, it's the exact time your dad always got up on Sundays to pray that his message would minister to the members of his congregation. Within an hour, all my sons and our best friends were in the room. We knelt around his bed and praised God for the years we'd had with this amazing man and asked for strength to carry on without him.

After a short time, I asked everyone to leave so I could say "goodbye." I cannot describe the feeling I had. Heaven seemed to envelop me as I praised God. I actually sensed a joy and the confidence that God was in control. In the years to follow, I realized how much I needed that experience to carry me through many challenging times with heart problems, financial decisions, a prodigal son, broken family relationships, and loneliness. God truly does lavish His love on us. "How great is the love the Father has lavished on us, that we should be called the children of God" (1 John 3:1).

In order to understand my being able to praise God at such a time, I must talk about Doug's and my strong love and partnership in ministry. Doug's growing up years entailed constant turmoil with his parents eventually divorcing and Doug's being sent to live with various relatives. A few years later, his mom met, fell in love with, and married a wonderful man. Doug had chosen a path of rebellion, smoking, drinking, choosing unruly companions, and eventually dropping out of school. At the age of sixteen, he was facing grand larceny charges and was in jail awaiting trial. His stepfather, an attorney, was able to help with bail and invited Doug to live with them. During that time, Doug's sister and brother-in-law had been attending a church in Liberal, Kansas. They had been invited by their eight-year-old daughter who was attending Vacation Bible School. Both parents accepted Christ as their savior and began to pray for Doug.

While out on bail, he finally agreed to their pleas to attend church with them. He felt that church was just for women and children, but as he expressed, "I just decided to go in order to 'get them off my back.'" As the pastor spoke that Sunday morning, Doug began to weep uncontrollably. Some would say he was just upset about the coming trial. We know the Holy Spirit was speaking to him and ultimately calling him into ministry. He tried to stop weeping, but when his sister handed him a tissue, he wept even more. "What would some of his friends who were there think?" The pastor walked down to him and asked, "Young man, would you like to come forward and receive Christ?"

Since Doug had not grown up attending any church regularly, he had no idea what the pastor was talking about, but responded, "I guess so." His story was that he knelt at the altar where the pastor asked him to confess his sins. Finally, these words made sense. He knew about "sin." The pastor asked him to visualize a blank piece of paper and to write his sins there and then to ask and receive God's forgiveness. When he finally looked up, he saw that he had been there for over an hour, though it seemed only a few minutes. Horror of horrors, the pastor asked him to give a testimony or tell of his experience. One must understand that Doug was extremely shy, but he stood and said, "I'm not really sure what just happened, but for the first time in eighteen years, I feel clean on the inside." Some might say that he simply felt an emotional release, but a total transformation had taken place. He went home and tossed his cigarettes and liquor. He faithfully attended church and began to study his Bible. This was the beginning of his favorite verse, "If any man is in Christ, he is a new creation. Old things are passed away. All things become new" (2 Cor. 5:17 NIV).

The pastor and family encouraged Doug by having him in their home often and teaching the scriptures. Through the process of the next year, Doug went back to complete high school with immense help from his step dad in math and English. By the end of that year, his pastor persuaded him to take the GED test and apply for admission to a Christian Liberal Arts college in Oklahoma. All was going well until Doug broke his leg playing softball in the summer. Discouragement set in; however, his family and church family kept praying and Doug was off to school on crutches. By this time, he knew God was calling him to ministry. His step dad, a wonderful Roman Catholic man suggested he take other classes "just in case" he changed his mind. He graciously agreed to pay for Doug's first year. Isn't God's grace abundant? He surrounds the righteous with His favor as with a shield (Ps. 5:12 NIV).

Here is where this spunky little girl from Texas appeared on the scene. When I was only six years old, my dad, age thirty-six, was killed in a trucking accident. My mother showed determination to keep us five children together by going back to school to earn her nursing degree. Unfortunately, she turned to drugs and alcohol to handle the stress. I often hid from her as she screamed obscenities and threw things. Over the years she remarried and had another child. As a young teen, I cared for my two younger brothers, cooked all meals, and cleaned the entire house while maintaining high marks in school and participating in my church youth group. Even though my mother was a high functioning alcoholic until later years, she did send us to church where we experienced love and a measure of peace. At the age of twelve, I accepted Jesus as my savior and at age thirteen, I accepted His call to a life of full-time ministry at our Dallas District Church camp in Scottsville, Texas. I began to pray as the Psalmist David in Psalm 25:5. "Guide me in your truth and teach me. For you are God, my Savior, and my hope is in you all day long."

Since I chose to attend a small Christian Liberal Arts College in Oklahoma, my mother was angry and asked me to leave our home the day I graduated from high school. My cousin and her husband invited me to live with them in Ft. Worth, Texas, where I secured employment with a huge natural gas company. I saved enough money to attend college in the fall. Even though I had earned two full tuition scholarships for secular schools, I knew I wanted to be in a place where I was more likely to prepare for ministry and to meet a Christian man. Not only did God provide for my financial needs through working in the college business office, I met the man of my dreams in October of my freshman year. After being introduced by an upperclassman, I returned to my dorm room and told my roommate that I had just met the man I would be marrying.

We both found it amusing that the upper classman told Doug how "good looking" I was since the upper classman was blind. When my roommate asked me how I could know Doug was the one, I simply replied, "How could I not know when I've been praying for God's leading and provision since I was twelve years of age?" At one of the youth camps I attended, the evangelist has us memorize Psalm 84:11. "For the Lord God is a sun and a shield; the Lord bestows favor (grace) and honor; no good thing does He withhold from those whose walk is blameless." Our meeting and dating were surely good things. We dated and were married two years later.

God continued to provide for us financially as Doug was elected to a position on the student council, which paid half his tuition and he received a Broadhurst ministerial scholarship for the other half. I continued to earn my honor scholarship and work in the business office. After graduation, we moved to Kansas where Doug was youth pastor and attended seminary. I taught middle school English. In the years to follow, we were blessed with three sons as we pastored in seven different churches. Even though I taught school for thirty of those years, we remained a ministry team. After Doug took an early retirement, I was able to go with him to the various churches where he was consulting and speaking.

My young friend, Marci, never had a warning of any kind that her spouse was ill. Her precious husband was killed instantly while driving a company truck. They had been married for only three years. My friend Kim awoke to her husband's lifeless body. He died of a heart attack at the young age of forty-six. I praise God for their strong testimonies and how God has carried them through...now twelve years later. Any time I am tempted to overly indulge in self-pity (confession is good for the soul), I praise God for those months that Doug and I had time to get ready... Well...try to get ready. One is never ready to lose a loved one. Of course we all have different stories; however, we all have so much in common. Our lives begin to drastically change when we become widows. We have so many decisions to make, and humanly, we have to make those decisions alone. Family and friends are there, but we feel so alone. We are widows who have a heavenly husband who gives grace to travel this journey.

Suggestions for Coping During the Days Before Death

1. If you are still employed, arrange some time off, if at all possible.
2. Take a break from church ministries as much as possible.
3. Make a list of ways people can help you when they ask in case your mind is fuzzy.

   a) Mow the lawn or take out the trash
   b) Pick up the children after school or take them to music lesson or sports practice. Have them take pictures also.
   c) Pick up needed items at store such as laundry detergent
   d) Mail bills, purchase stamps, or send needed correspondence
   e) Place food in your freezer
   f) Run the sweeper
   g) Help with animals
   h) Return or pick up library books

4. Have a notebook or computer with you to take notes about questions for the doctor.
5. Write scripture promises on three-by-five cards to read and pray over and over.
6. Make a list of people to call if/when death occurs
7. Have phone numbers and names for pastor, funeral home, places for cancellations.
8. Make sure your wills and power of health attorney are all up to date
9. Tell your adult children where things are such all passwords and how to access any accounts as needed
10. Have a journal to express your feelings.

11. Make sure you know all of your husband's passwords.

12. Make sure you know where important documents are, *especially your marriage certificate* (more about his in chapter 2).

13. Take time to exercise even if just a stroll around the hospital. Studies have shown that exercise may be as helpful as some medications

14. Take care of your health by eating properly so you will be strong for what lies ahead.

15. Organize your photographs or videos in case they are needed for the funeral.

16. Above all, saturate yourself with God's word so that you can stay calm as you hope and trust in Him. When your loved one's time comes, God will provide the right people to guide you such as your pastor, the hospital staff, funeral director, friends, or financial consultants.

2

Grace for the Funeral

Having lost so many loved ones—my dad when I was six, my two brothers who died in their forties, my grandparents, my precious mother-in-law and close friend, my mother, and many parishioners—I thought I would be ready for Doug's funeral. Of course I knew the basic steps. Since Doug died in the hospital, the personnel there took care of calling the coroner. I gave them the name of the funeral home and pastor from my previous list. You might be thinking, "Wow, she was calm." Not! I was breathing deeply and praying continually. God's grace and provision showed up in so many ways with the first being that our best friends were at our home running the household, taking in food, making lists for thank-you notes, cleaning, answering the phone, doorbell...anything needed.

Doug's best friend, Jim, is a mortician and told us exactly what was needed. I cry as I write this to think that Jim wanted to get Doug ready for the funeral. "Oh, Jim," I exclaimed, "I would not want you to have to do that." With tears in his eyes, he gently but firmly replied, "I consider it a great honor to get this godly man, my friend, ready for his last service here on earth." Not only did he do a remarkable job of dressing Doug, he organized and set up the visitation for about six hundred people saving me at least $1,000.

Since Doug had suffered from a rare autoimmune disease, we formerly had decided to donate his body for science; however, God had different plans. Doug passed before we could fill in the necessary documents. Seeing him in the casket brought wonderful closure for our family and the over five hundred people who came. Even though we were experiencing near blizzard weather in Michigan that February, people came from several states. The evening before the funeral, we stood for hours welcoming people from our community where Doug was in Rotary and other civic organizations, people from other churches, from the school system where I had taught, college students, and the many people from our own church. I'm so glad we had the open casket. I know that is not for everyone; however, in this situation, the people whose lives he'd so affected needed to see him one more time. His peaceful aura brought comfort to our grieving souls. He seemed to be calling out from his coffin, "'Keep walking in the light as He is in the light' (1 John 1:7 NIV). Enjoy the journey. God is the great healer. He has allowed me go home. We can meet again."

At the service the next day, there was standing room only even though the snow had continued to fall. Doug had told me who he wanted to participate in his service, which included several of his former associate pastors. The music was beautiful from several of our former worship leaders. The congregation sang, "It is Well With My Soul" and "Great is Thy Faithfulness." With his wonderful sense of humor, Doug would have especially loved the ending song. Since a large number of Doug's ancestors were Scottish, my middle son, Vince, wanted "Amazing Grace" to be played on bagpipes at the burial; however, the weather did not cooperate so the bag pipe player decided to play in the sanctuary right when the casket was being rolled out. No one had thought to inform our former worship leader who was playing the piano so beautifully when this loud bag pipe bellowed out the chords. Even in all my grief, I couldn't help but smile as she nearly jumped out of her skin. To this day, we still laugh. I imagined Doug looking down with that great smile and deep belly laugh. God surely must have a sense of humor to make us laugh even at this heartbreaking time.

I felt like I was handling things fairly well those first few days, but in retrospect, I realize that I felt rushed. My three sons were doing their best to help me and suggested the service be in three days. That seemed like a long time until we had to get all the pictures ready, make calls, figure out who was going to sleep where, what to wear, and how to set up the church. On one occasion, the funeral home had informed me that I needed to have the obituary ready for online and the picture boards ready by the next day. I put the guys and their families to work on the pictures while my professor and computer savvy daughter-in-law helped me with the writing.

Laughter erupted from the basement where my three sons were going through the pictures. When I went to check, they had made little progress. In retrospect, I realize this was a good time; however, as in the story of Mary and Martha in the Bible, somebody had to get things in order. Feeling a little irritated, I asked God to help me. About that time, the doorbell rang to welcome one of our former extremely organized and crafty associates who had gone to high school with my sons. In no time at all, she had the guys organized and all the pictures placed on the boards. God kept reminding me of Philippians 4:6. "Don't worry about anything; instead, pray about everything" (NLT). He truly cares about every detail of whatever we need to accomplish.

Now it was time for everyone to figure out what to wear. Guess who got to watch the grandsons while the couples shopped? Again, my attitude was a little less than sanctimonious. I really did not have time to even think about my attire which was probably for the best since I would begin to face financial issues the next week. I'm not sure others talk to their deceased loved one, but I looked at his picture on the dresser and exclaimed, "Well, Doug, you have very handsome, well-dressed sons and their wives, but I'm not so sure about your wife." I could just imagine his saying, as he often did, "You are the most beautiful woman in the world." I would always tell him that I knew that was not true, but to keep it up. I really missed that after he died. I would get ready each day and wonder how he would like what I had chosen to wear or how I styled my hair. Now I have his picture on the top of the chest of drawers. I imagine his smiling and saying, "Look'n good." My whimsical daughter-in-law offered to FaceTime me each morning to do the same. I expressed my appreciation but told her that probably would not work.

After the amazing celebration service, the church had a huge dinner, but many people wanted to get home before more snow arrived. Consequently, our family ate ham sandwiches for weeks. People also brought entire meals for two more weeks. I quickly began to think about thank-you notes. Now, I am not a note writer but have always disciplined myself to do so as the people in our churches have always been so gracious and generous to us. A great idea came to me. I'm really not sure if someone told me this or it was from God. I took pictures of the foods brought and all the flower arrangements with the little cards so that when I wrote the notes I could describe what people had sent. Many gave financial gifts for our grandchildren's college. I did not even try to write the notes until two weeks later after everyone had gone home. Once again, I began to pray my favorite verse" "'Oh Lord, you know I am weak, but your strength is made perfect in that weakness' (2 Cor. 12:9). Please help me to accomplish this task." I sat down and completed every note that day. Once again, God's wonderful grace lifted me.

I have listened to the CD from the service over and over. During the service, we played a "tape" of Doug's rich base voice singing, "Oh Glorious Love" by John W. Peterson.

> In my darkness Jesus found me, touched my
> eyes and made me see
> Though sin's chains that long had bound
> me
> Gave me life and liberty
>
> (Chorus) Oh glorious love of Christ my
> Lord divine
> That made him stoop to save a soul like
> mine
> Through all my days and then in heaven
> above

My song will silence never. I'll worship him
forever and praise him for his glorious love.

(Verse 2) Oh amazing truth to ponder. He
whom angels close attend.
Lord of heaven God's son, what wonder.
He became the sinner's friend.

These words were truly his testimony. During the first year of
my grieving, I would sit by the fire almost every evening with tears in
my eyes while listening to his deep, rich base voice, being reassured
that God's glorious love would continue to keep me. My precious
pastor son, who is also a licensed marriage and family therapist, was
always hinting that I should cry more. He didn't see those nightly
tears, but God did and they brought wonderful healing. We all grieve
in such different ways, but God is faithful to bring us through as we
cry out to Him. On various occasions during their youth, one of
my sons would call to tell about a time of discouragement such as a
tough test, a relationship gone bad, or financial needs. I would listen,
of course, and remind them that it was okay to "cry out to God as the
psalmist did." Now, I needed to say those words myself from Psalm
18:1–3: "The Lord is my rock, my fortress and my deliverer; my God
is my rock, in whom I take refuge. He is my shield and the horn of
my salvation, my stronghold. I call to the Lord, who is worthy of my
praise."

I am so thankful for the time Doug and I had to prepare for his
home going. Even with that, so many things came up that we had
not considered. Countless last-minute decisions had to be made such
as "Who will sit where?" and the order of service. My adult children
helped me every step of the way. As we stood in that long receiving
line, my feet began to hurt and I wondered how many more times I
could say "thank-you" when people said, "I'm sorry." At times, I felt
that I was comforting them. Now that I look back, I see their good
hearts and am so careful about what I say to the grieving person.
Many of my widow friends have not been so privileged. Their spouses
were taken suddenly or their families were not supportive. Some did

not have great family or church support or financial means. During the funeral, their minds might have been racing to think how they would meet obligations.

What seemed like an ordinary day turned into disaster for Gayle. When she arrived home from work that afternoon, her husband, Lee, was laughing as he told her he had been craving peanut butter sandwiches all day and if she would like one to enjoy on the way. (He knew she didn't really care for peanut butter.) While driving down the four-lane highway, enjoying their usual loving banter, Gayle suddenly had to grab the wheel to keep the car from swerving into the other lane. After running into a mailbox along the side of the road, she was able to pull the car to a stop. When she was finally able to look at Lee, his eyes were closed and his head flopped back onto the head rest. Cars were flying by as she frantically waved for help. In desperation, she stood right in front of a truck that was pulling out of the driveway by the mailbox. At first, the man was angry and yelled for her to get out of the way. He finally complied when she begged him to help her lift Lee's body out of the car and away from the traffic.

Gayle knew that her husband was gone even before the ambulance arrived. Within an hour, she had called us, her pastors and friends. I'll never forget the look on her face as we went into the room. She kept telling us, "He's gone. He's gone and I didn't get to say goodbye." My husband went in with her to see the body after the staff had completed preparations. What a total shock! Even though we were sad because they were our close friends, I could not conceive her grief until after I had lost my own husband. With God's grace and strength, Gayle was able to move through all the arrangements and the service. She even sang a solo, "It Is Well with My Soul." Her deep faith held her steady and still does twenty years later.

For several years, Mary lived with the possibility of her husband's dying. He was a brittle diabetic who gave himself shots daily or more often as needed. Most days, he seemed his wonderful self of what I refer to as a "gentle giant." He was really tall and handsome with a love for family and friends, especially children. Having taught elementary school for thirty plus years, he was a magnet for them.

The last time we visited them in Pennsylvania, our youngest son, age ten, sat totally spellbound as Jack told him stories of all the beautiful buildings in downtown Pittsburg.

Due partly to health reasons, Jack took retirement in his fifties but continued to work part-time and to get projects completed around their beautiful New England home. Mary was still working in a doctor's office a few miles away. She would often check on him via phone or he would go by the office to take her to lunch or out to coffee…those wonderful things "empty nesters" get to do. The week that he passed away was two days after Christmas…wonderful times with family. After everyone left, Mary and Jack were ready to sleep in. Early the next morning, Jack got up saying he could not sleep, so went downstairs. When Mary awakened a few hours later, she went downstairs ready for an adventure to the coffee shop where Jack spent considerable time working on his computer and talking to people about his faith as opportunity allowed. Jack was not ready to go and asked if it would be all right for him to take a little nap before they went. She went up with him and stayed while he took a shower and got ready to lie down.

Mary slipped downstairs to read and relax. As she sat downstairs on the couch, she could hear that Jack was not sleeping. She could hear his telephone conversation with his cousin, Ron, who had offered to give Jack one of his kidneys a few months earlier. True to Jack's loving and giving nature, he told his cousin that he was fearful that it would cause problems for him. Jack also knew that his cousin was having some spiritual issues. On that day, two days after Christmas, Jack told Ron that he would accept the kidney as long as he assured him that he would recommit his life to God. Those were the last words Mary heard from her precious husband as she drifted off for a little nap downstairs.

In an hour or so, Mary decided to go upstairs to check on Jack. A stillness and complete quietness enveloped her as she crept up the stairs. When Jack did not respond, she pulled back the covers to discover that he had made his trip to heaven. When the ER people arrived, they said that he had been gone for over an hour. Of course, Mary was distraught to think that she had been dozing on the couch right downstairs. She asked herself why she could not have been with him when he passed. How could she have known? Jack often took little times of rest. Her pastor and friends tried to assure her that that he passed just as he was supposed to.

It was almost as if he knew his time was near. Their son-in-law told Mary that on Christmas day, Jack had sat down beside him and said, "I want to thank you for being the most wonderful son-in-law there could be. You take care of my daughter and your family so well. I know if anything happens to me, you will be there for all of them and for Mary." Perhaps Jack went upstairs that day because he did not want Mary to see him really ill. Only eternity will reveal. The cousin could not understand why Jack had finally agreed to take his kidney and then he passed before it could happen. Mary explained God's plan and love for him. He did recommit his life and is now living a strong Christian life.

Surely, those and other thoughts were going through Mary's mind as she sat through not one, but two funeral services. True to Jack's steady, sure and loving nature, he had planned every detail of the service complete with speakers, Bible verses, places, and music. Since their burial plots were in their hometown of Pittsburg, Pennsylvania, she was concerned about the time frame and the travel from the east coast through near blizzard type weather. Even in her grief, she was thinking about Jack's ninety-four-year-old mother who would be coming from Florida. The month before Jack died, she and he had agreed to memorize the verse from Isaiah 41:10. They had it on a special card placed with a magnet on their refrigerator. "So do not fear, for I am with you; do not be dismayed for I am your God. I will strengthen you and help you; I will uphold you with my righteous right hand."

I'm pretty sure I was the first person Mary called to ask for prayer the day Jack passed. I was deeply humbled, yet having just lost my husband the year before and still in a state of deep grief, I was almost speechless. I sent up one of those SOS prayers. "Help, Lord. You know how much I loved this man too. He was one of my husband's closest friends and Mary was mine." With God's amazing strength and many tears, I began to call on the name of the Lord, our strong tower. "The name of the Lord is a strong tower. The righteous run to it and they are safe" (Prov. 18:10 NIV).

We ran into that "strong tower" together and talked many times throughout the next year. Even though I was devastated, I was strengthened by helping Mary. I knew that calling her and other widows was going to be a great part of my ministry for the next years. In 2 Corinthians, Paul tells us, "The God of all comfort comforts us, in all our troubles so that we can comfort those in any trouble with the comfort we ourselves have received from God," (2 Cor. 1:3b–4 NIV). I have a confession. "Not too many people called me after the first few weeks and I was a little hurt." The Lord spoke to me about how many times I had not called and comforted others because I did not understand their true grief. Another of my widow friends apologized for not calling me as I had called her. I was able to say with complete truth, "You did not understand because you had not lost your sweetheart at that point."

Teresa's very calm and patient husband, Rick, loved to go for long bike rides and repair things around their home. A few weeks before, on his last bike ride of fifteen miles, he had felt a little dizzy so went for a complete physical where he received a clean bill of health. The doctor sent him on his way to their winter home in Florida. Rick was outside working on the hurricane windows for about an hour. Feeling thirsty, he went in and expressed feelings of nausea and weakness. Teresa called 911. As instructed, she tried CPR between screaming, "Don't you dare leave me!" He did leave, though, and she was there in Florida away from all her children and family. Her one daughter was working in a foreign country, and her other daughter and family were in the Northeast. Thankfully, Teresa had great neighbors who helped her call the family and make arrangements to return to their home in Pennsylvania.

Completely devastated and surprised, Teresa began to make funeral arrangement with the help of her pastor and family. She had two weeks before her daughter could be back in the States so she used that time to prepare a beautiful life story bulletin. Her scrapbooking skills really came in handy, enabling her to focus. Since Rick had requested to be cremated, Teresa was able to take his ashes back to Pennsylvania…thus sparing the expense of embalming and other normal funeral expenses. The service was a beautiful testimony of a life totally given to Rick's wonderful Savior. Many who attended said they received a glimpse of what heaven must be like as they listened to the National Christian Choir in which Rick had sung for years and listened to so many testimonies of how Rick had touched their lives. Teresa remembers thinking how embarrassed Rick would have been to hear all those accolades, but they brought great comfort and closure for her and her adult children and grandchildren.

Doug's celebration service was truly beautiful and uplifting. My three sons each paid tribute to their dad, former associates spoke and sang and people sent letters. One that encouraged me immensely was from Doug's former college roommate. He had a special section that expressed my love and help for Doug's success in the ministry. I'm not sure I would ever have thought to do that for someone who was grieving. His words gave me courage to face new challenges and trust God even more. Life goes on and more problems come, but I am convinced as the Apostle Paul in Romans 8:38–39, "Nothing can ever separate us from God's love. Neither death nor life, neither angels nor demons neither the present or the future, nor any powers, neither height or depth, nor anything else in all creation, will be able to separate us from the love of God that is in Christ Jesus our Lord."

Suggestions/Helps for Funeral

1. If you have a close relationship with a pastor or deeply spiritual friend, talk with them about arrangements.
2. Sit quietly and think about what your loved one enjoyed. Write down things you want shared at the service such as his life story and other stories dear to your heart
3. Do not allow others to dictate the place or time of the service.
4. Your funeral director will help you order death certificates.
5. Make copies of all records such as life insurance, banking, car titles, bills to pay, passwords of your husband's and yours.
6. You might be able to save money if you have visitation at your church with church volunteers ushering.
7. If you are having your loved one's body cremated, you may choose your own guest book, thank-you notes, picture boards, and videos.
8. Get help in organizing pictures. A friend might be more objective.
9. If your loved one had life insurance, call the company as soon as possible. They will ask for the policy number and a death certificate.
10. Choose appropriate clothes for your loved one.
11. Choose appropriate yet comfortable clothes for yourself for the visitation and service. I chose an outfit that my husband always liked. Comfortable shoes are a must.
12. If there is a dinner given by your church or friends, be sure to have someone take pictures and make a list for thank-you notes. Have someone take pictures of any flowers with the tags. If possible, ask someone to make sure all addresses are on the cards.
13. Decide whether you will speak at the service. I chose not to since all three of my sons spoke as well as many of our

former associate pastors. Later, I had some regrets because I wished I had shared how much I loved him.

14. Designate someone to take pictures and make sure the video camera is working.

3

Making Financial and Other Major Decisions

The promise found in Philippians 4:19 has carried me through many difficult situations. "He will supply all your needs according to His riches in Christ Jesus." When I went to college with only $180 and a few little scholarships, God provided with more scholarships, employment, and student loans that I didn't even have to repay since I secured a teaching job in a lower socioeconomic area. Our first ministry assignment in Kansas was close to the seminary from which Doug graduated. He drove fifty miles one way every day while pastoring. Again God provided scholarships and a full-time teaching job for me.

After Doug took an early retirement, we thought we had our home sold; however, the buyers backed out at the signing table. Right after this, the market crashed, making it a buyer's market. Since we had secured a bridge loan with the home we were building, we had to continue making large payments on both homes for a period of three years. Thankfully, after that extended time, both homes sold within a six-month period. We probably lost $300,000 on the two houses by the time we sold, but we had enough money left for a down payment on a lovely condo right down the street from our son and his family. We had gone through nearly all of our retirement, so when

Doug passed away, I had to rely on a moderate life insurance, my small teacher retirement from the state of Michigan, Doug's small retirement from pastoring for forty years, and Social Security. Please understand, I am very thankful for my eleven years of teaching in Michigan, the only state where we stayed long enough for me to be vested and eligible for amazing health insurance. Unfortunately, Doug's retirement for forty years of ministry is small; however, I give thanks that it buys groceries for a few weeks each month.

One of the first things I had to do was go to the Social Security office to fill out necessary forms to receive Doug's benefit payment since it was the higher of the two. Panic set in as I realized all payments were stopped until paperwork went through. Due to the circumstances mentioned above, I had about $400 on which to survive until this happened. Moving on autopilot, I got what I thought were all the necessary documents together and made my way to the Social Security office. Much to my surprise, on that early Monday morning, the line of people needing help was out the door. After waiting quite patiently for two hours, I was called to the window. The first thing the clerk asked for was my marriage license. I had no idea that I would need it, and not a clue as to where it might be. As tears sprang to my eyes, the compassionate clerk told me to make an appointment; however, I could not get in for two weeks. What was I supposed to do for money in the meantime? As I often do, I sent up one of those SOS prayers. "Oh Lord, you are able to do immeasurably more than I can ask or imagine" (Eph. 3:20 NIV).

Just as I was walking away, the clerk called me back to inform me that the lines were much smaller on Wednesdays. You know I was there, bright and early the next Wednesday and was called almost immediately. The clerk took me back to her private office and assured me that all would go through within a week. She even gave me her personal phone number in case I hadn't heard anything within that time. Wow! God did do more than I could imagine according to His glorious riches in Christ Jesus. I began to praise with the words from Psalm 63: "Because your love is better than life, my lips will glorify you. I will praise you as long as I live, and in your name, I will lift my hands" (verses 3–4 NIV). I waited until I got to the car to lift my hands.

Finding the marriage license before I went back to the Social Security office was quite the challenge. As I sat down at the filing cabinet, I thought, *This will be a piece of cake since Doug was so meticulous about filing.* Not so much this time! First, I looked under the letter "M" for marriage license. Not there. Then on to letter "L" for license. "W" for wedding. Not there. My prayers became more intense as I decided to start at the beginning of the file and look at every paper. Wow! Who would ever think it was filed under certificates with birth, wedding, and dedication of children? Believe me, I began to tell all my friends to make sure they know where this document is. Many have told me they had no ideas they would need it should their loved one pass.

While I was waiting on the Social Security money to come, I applied for the life insurance money knowing that I would need it soon to pay funeral expenses and other obligations. The money came within two weeks...another miracle. Our mortician friend guided me through the process. When I look back, I am amazed at God's strength, direction, and grace. Being in a fog, I just methodically went through my list. One thing was to check on the car that Doug leased for business travel. The Toyota dealership where we had leased dismissed the rest of the six months left on the lease, which gave me an extra $240 per month (immeasurably more than I imagined). I needed to sell our other car, which was a 2003 Ford Taurus with 200,000 miles on it. Even though Doug and I went over all paperwork and monthly bills, I didn't know where to look for the title. It wasn't in the car glovebox or in the folder marked, "Automobile." Should I look under "F" for Ford or "T" for Taurus? There it was right under "F."

One of the ladies in my Bible study told me her husband loved to sell cars for people even though he is often traveling as an executive for a large Michigan-based company. He told me I could use his number and he would show it and let them drive it from where I was able to park it in the church parking lot (one of the benefits of being the pastor's mom). On the second day the car was parked there, I noticed a gentleman and his teenage daughter were looking at it. I felt really safe since many people were at church so I pulled up and introduced myself. After driving the car, he made a nice cash offer and arranged to do all the paperwork the next day…just one more way God provided for me. Now I had to make decisions about a newer car. Our former associate pastor, now pastor of that church, loved to look at cars. He immediately lined up great used ones for me. I will tell more about the anxiety over purchasing a car for the first time in a later chapter.

One of the more unpleasant decisions we widows have to make while in that state of shock is choosing a headstone. Driving to the granite place a few miles away gave me time to reflect on the one my mother had chosen for my dad when I was a little girl. It had a picture on it. That's one thing I knew I wanted. I also wanted it to convey Doug's testimony of a transformed life. My confidence in choosing the right marker melted way as I walked through all the samples. The woman in charge invited me to look through a book and the prices. "Overwhelmed" does not adequately describe my feelings. I should have had one of my sons go with me, but I didn't want to burden them with more grief. I calmly (on the outside) expressed my gratitude and told her I was not ready to make a decision.

Shortly after I arrived home, the funeral director called to ask if I wanted to come in to look at pictures of headstones with different fonts and wording. Surprisingly, the prices were lower and included in the funeral bill. Should I choose one with both our names on it and leave the date for my passing open? My thirteen-year-old grandson exclaimed, "Please don't do that, Gramma. I don't want to go to the cemetery and see your name on a tombstone." Guess I had never thought about that but decided to go with a single stone with Doug's picture and the words of his favorite verse, "If any man is in Christ, he is a new creation. Old things are passed away and all things become new" (2 Cor. 5:17 NIV). Thankfully, the funeral home took care of all the details. More grace!

Within a few weeks after the funeral, I knew I needed to send thank-you notes. My first were for the wonderful people who helped with the funeral like the piano player, the pastors, vocalists, etc.

Within a few days, they had all sent the checks back that I had mailed to them, exclaiming that they would never take money for doing something so beautiful. Other friends from college days sent checks of one and two hundred dollars. How did they know the social security checks and life insurance had not arrived? Every time money was getting low, a check mysteriously appeared from friends, rebates, tax refunds. What an amazing God we serve! "Are there any God's like you, oh Lord. There are no gods like you. You are amazingly powerful, wonderfully holy, a worker of miracles" (Exod. 15:11 NCV).

Yes, Doug passed in February and taxes had to be prepared. Actually, I always hire a CPA, but I had to get all the documents ready. My well-organized husband had all the worksheets from previous years, which made it a little easier. When I realized I was eligible for so many deductions, I realized again how God was providing for me. I had made a list of how much less would be coming in each month with losing some of Doug's retirement, my social security, and his speaking engagements. Then I created a list of fewer expenses like fewer groceries, entertainment expenses, doctor bills, etc. God continued to show His favor (grace) even when I had felt afraid and had experienced several meltdowns. Psalm 145:9 holds true. "The Lord is good to all; he has compassion on all he has made" (NIV).

One of the first things on my list was to update the will. Yes, making a list is so helpful when your brain is foggy and you feel overwhelmed. Having had a local lawyer write our wills and power of health attorney made it easier. Since we had few assets, our lawyer wrote the will so that our estate would not go into probate court. All I had to do was call the lawyer to update names and addresses of our sons and explain how any money from life insurance or the sale of the home in case of my death would be divided among my three sons. My feelings of intimidation were quickly eased as the lawyer explained everything to me and to my oldest son. Copies of the Power of Health Attorney and other documents are safely stored in a place known to my oldest son who was designated as the executor of my will. Having them in a fire-proof lock box puts our minds at ease.

What a blessing that Doug had life insurance that partially made up for all the money we had lost on the houses. Fortunately, the funeral home was willing to wait until I received the check (more grace). My mortician friend suggested that I not disclose the amount of the insurance until after the funeral home had written the bill. As soon as I received the check, I paid them and any bills that we had. This was the first time I had written checks for such large amounts. With trembling hands, I wrote all those zeros. Yes, the funeral was expensive even with all my discounts...$8,000. That left half of the money to invest. The financial advisor explained everything to me and my three sons. The amount was modest but enough for me to draw interest each month to balance my budget.

I encountered some difficulty in having the name on the title of our home changed to my name only. Of course, I sent the death certificate and a letter. Another month went by with no change. I felt it was important to have it in my name only, in case something happened to me and my sons would need to sell the home. I called and was assured that the change would be made, and of course, they went all through how sorry they were for his passing. It can be a little awkward. Two more months went by with the house still being in both our names. Finally, after two more phone calls, the work was completed. A few months later, when I needed a home equity loan for a new furnace and updates, my loan officer assured me how good it was that I had done this. Yes, I had to make more decisions such as, "Should I get a new furnace? What kind of flooring? What is the best deal, color, product?" Doug and I had always made these decisions together with his being so much better at it. What process did I use to decide?

First, I prayed for wisdom as in James 1:5. (NIV): "If any of you should need wisdom, let them ask of God, who gives generously to all without finding fault." I really like that last part because no matter how many times I ask, I know He still gives. Then I did research. According to what stage of grief you are in, you might be saying, "I wouldn't even be able to concentrate on any type of research." My suggestion would be to just wait, if possible. The next things I did was make a list of all pros and cons of the needed project, showed them to my son and one of wonderful handymen from our church. I always took a few weeks to decide. Did I ever make a wrong choice?

Well, yes. I bought a nice coffee table for my living room and had to trade it three times. Of course, I couldn't trade the floors or the furnace, so I was so much more careful. Putting in the new furnace has saved me more than $100 monthly. I try to put that toward the home equity loan each month even though it is so tempting to do a little retail therapy.

Driving twenty miles south to the town where we had last pastored was difficult for me. We loved our bank there so much that we continued to do business with them even though we had moved about twenty miles north. I felt so alone as I walked into the bank and so afraid that I would lose it in front of these people. Since we had lived in that community for fifteen years, the tellers all knew and loved Doug. He did most of the banking for our family, and one of the tellers told me that it always made her day when he came in on Mondays to deposit his check or to take care of church business. Of course, I did break down but was ushered into a private office where I signed all the proper papers to have my son's name on the list in case of emergencies. Nellie, the bank officer talked to me for an hour. We rejoiced at our common faith in God. She passed away one month later from a heart attack. So glad I made that trip to the bank when I did.

One of the hardest decisions to make is what to do with your husband's clothes. All of my sons are bigger than their dad; however, they went through the ties, hats, socks, housecoats, etc., and took what they wanted. Doug had at least thirty suits, many shirts and sweaters, and of course, his beloved Dallas Cowboy and Pittsburg Steeler shirts. Once again, I was at a loss as to what to do with all these nice things. With the prompting of the Holy Spirit, I decided to wait a while. I had been trying to comfort a couple from our last ministry assignment. Their eighteen-year-old son had struggled with drug addiction and had recently been through rehab and seemed to be on the right track. While traveling back from visiting one of his friends, he was killed instantly when his truck slid into a tree. I went to their home and talked with them on the phone several times. Four months later, I asked if they would come to my home for a little time of rest...just to get away from all the publicity surrounding their son's death. I did not feel strong emotionally but relied on the verse from 2 Corinthians 9:8: "God is able to make all grace abound to you so that in all things, at all times, having all that you need, you will abound in every good work" (NIV).

Amazingly, they did accept my invitation. Since the accident had occurred only a few months before, I knew they must still be in somewhat of a state of shock. The husband was a builder and really good at any type of "fix it" project. He noticed my sliding door was really hard to open and close and made a noise when sliding. He assured me that doing things helped him relax and work through his grief. During the course of our conversation, he mentioned that they were going to shop for a coat on their way home. Immediately, I thought about Doug's two beautiful wool coats that he often wore when officiating at graveside ceremonies in the frigid Michigan winters. I didn't want to offend Dan by offering but felt a little prompting to ask, "Would you be offended or feel strange to wear one of Doug's coats?"

Through his tears, he responded, "I would be so honored to wear Pastor's coat." It was a perfect fit in more ways than one. More wisdom and grace bestowed so graciously!

A week later my friend Susan was talking about her son-in-law getting his internship at a Chicago hospital. Her daughter and he had been in residence at a hospital in Puerto Rico. Into my mind popped, "He will need warm clothes and even suits." Again I asked if she thought he would be offended to wear some of Doug's sweaters, coats, and suits. Within an hour, she called back saying her son-in-law was elated. That next Sunday afternoon, they came to my home, and Justin tried everything on and was like a kid in a candy shop. He kept saying, "I can't believe I have the privilege of wearing Pastor Doug's clothes." I feel so honored and am so thankful for God's provision. Now that he is a full-fledged doctor in a southern state, he may not be using them, but I marvel at God's plan for that time both in my life and theirs. God's grace was still abounding.

My husband was the neatest man I've ever known. He kept all of his socks and underwear folded perfectly in three full drawers. My boys and some of our friends took some of the dress socks, but who would want all those white socks and T-shirts? In the summer after Doug had passed in February, one of my children wanted to have a garage sale and asked if they could use my garage since it was a better location. I put a few things out but never thought about all that underwear. A lady came by who worked with prison ministries. She asked if I had any socks. Wow! Do I? She was so thankful as I gave her three bags full as I'm thinking, *Wouldn't Doug be so happy that he was still giving and loving to help others?* Remember in the first chapter when I told about his having been in jail before he became a Christian?

I did keep some of his favorite things, and I actually go to the closet sometimes and just hug his soft flannel jacket and shirt. My teenage grandsons love wearing Papa's housecoat and his ball caps. Going through all his things six months after he died was something I had to do by myself. Some widows want someone to help, and some don't want to part with things for a much longer period of time. Had God not arranged the circumstances written above, I might have kept things longer. I do know that I had a feeling of satisfaction that Doug was still giving and that he would be so happy.

That first year was so busy with all of these things and now I needed a different car. Should I get a new one, lease one, or purchase a used one? My husband's former associate pastor loved car shopping so he helped me look. I found one on line that was a few years old with only 57,000 miles. Pastor Mel came to the car place to look things over and to drive it. Two of my sons also drove it. I truly appreciated all the support, but I went alone to the dealership to sign the papers. I had never purchased a car before. Being so fulfilled in my teaching and children's ministry at church, I was happy to have Doug choose any car we purchased. He would just drive up and ask me if I liked it, and I would say, "If you like, I will too." Actually, I wanted a bright blue convertible but knew that would never go over.

My son did offer to go with me to do the paperwork; however, I thought the process would be relatively simple. I would just use part of the life insurance money, write the check, and be on the way. The salesperson kept having to leave the room to check on various things concerning insurance. Panic would creep into my soul with thoughts of *What am I doing? This is a used car. What if it breaks down? Should I purchase a warranty?* I was on the verge of tears as I wrote the down payment check for $8,000 with butterflies in my stomach. That night, I couldn't sleep because I had not purchased the warranty for the Hybrid with its $4,000 battery. Where was my trust? Swallowed in grief, no doubt. The next morning, I went back by the dealership and purchased the warranty. My mind was much more at ease even though I wish now that I had not spent the money. We widows do make errors, but we learn and survive. The car did amazing, and I was able to sell it a few years later for $4,000.

Having a different car meant talking to the insurance people. When I saw the amount, I began to call around for a comparison. Because of my great record of no accidents or tickets (believe me, God's grace kept me from some tickets I deserved), Triple AAA gave me a deal that was not even half what I was paying. The lady at the office of my old insurance actually cried because I was leaving their company because we had been with them so long. I explained that I really appreciated her kind words, but unless they could lower the rates, I could not afford it. This whole process took several hours on the phone and filling out a lot of papers. Throughout the process, I continually called out to God that I needed wisdom and patience. God so graciously brought to my mind the promise in Isaiah 42:16b, "I will turn the darkness into light and make the rough places smooth."

Doug had always taken care of any home improvement projects. Wanting my approval and thanks, he always explained what he was doing, but I guess I didn't pay enough attention. A few months before, on a day that he felt better, we had chosen new vanities and paint colors for the bathrooms, changed light fixtures, and chosen new flooring for the kitchen and baths. After he passed, I hired an electrician to install the fans and lights. Once again, my mind was racing: "Who should I call? Will I be taken advantage of? How do I know if he will do a good job?" After confessing my sin of fretting (Psalm 37 instructs us to fret not), I remembered a young man who had worked on our last home, but I didn't have any contact information. I'm so thankful that God cares about all of our little details.

The very next day, I called our former contractor and he gave me the information. I'm pretty sure the young man gave me a good deal. For $1,200, he put in all the electrical sockets in the unfinished basement, put in three ceiling fans and three light fixtures.

Incidentally, that basement is now finished...another of God's wonderful provisions. Doug and I had great friends from one of our former pastorates. The men were both expert handymen and semi-retired. Before Doug passed, they had come up several times to help us move into the condo and to begin working on the basement. In April, after Doug died in February, the wife of one of the guys called to ask me if I would like for them to come up to finish the basement. Accepting this wonderful gift was indeed humbling because I knew I couldn't afford to hire a contractor. When they came up a few weeks later, we girls spent our time shopping and cooking while they put in a ceiling, did Sheetrock, and put in a half bath. Wow! All I had to pay for were the supplies. The guy who did the ceiling, which looks beautiful, told me afterward that he had never done a ceiling and had been up half the night watching YouTube.

Many people at Doug's funeral expressed their desire to help in any way they could; however, I truly have a difficult time asking. One of the men in our local church, Jim, retired early and is always helping people with odd jobs. At that time, his wife was not retired, but she encouraged him to help. She would even come over in the evenings to see what he had accomplished. They helped with the basement project and came for dinner in the evening with the other two couples. One day I told him that he was really going to be blessed and he asked why? I replied, "The Bible does say to take care of the widows." He grinned and said, "You are really milking this, aren't you?" Of course, we were kidding each other, but he and his wife, Kathy are a blessing. Other projects he has completed are hanging pictures above the stairs, installing new vanities, building a new cabinet above the microwave he installed and completing the office room downstairs. John 1:16 reminds me, "From the fullness of His grace, we (I) have received one blessing after another."

Making decisions on all these things was far out of my comfort zone, but I had more to make. The furnace in my condo was thirty years old and my electric/gas bill was over $300 per month during the winter. Not only did I need a furnace and hot water heater, I needed more flooring and countertops for the kitchen. I did not want to use the life insurance money that I had invested because I was using the interest to balance my budget. A home equity loan seemed to be the answer…another first for me. After much prayer and several visits to the bank to fill out scads of paperwork, I secured the loan and began making more decisions. Things went great for the furnace and the flooring. The kitchen work was another story.

Unfortunately, I had secured the services of one of our "big box" stores who contract out the jobs. The right hand surely did not know what the left hand was doing. They would promise to call or come and not show up even after my calling. Of course, I diligently kept notes in my home repair notebook. Finally, I went to the head person at the store who had sold me on their services. She got things rolling; however, the process still took three months longer than they had promised and the final amount was $2,000 more than their estimate. Guess I had not read the fine print well enough, but I learned so much. Even in our mistakes, God uses us to help others. By the time the job was finished, I had the privilege of leading one of the workers to the Lord. He actually began to talk to me about "church."

A week earlier, our community had experienced a mass shooting. This young man discovered that he had gone to college with the shooter. He was pretty shaken and said the first thing he thought to do was to attend church, but he had issues and could I help him to get a different perspective. Now, by this time, I had made connections with this young man by baking cookies and helping him with one of his children's schoolwork. I sent up one of those SOS prayers as I thought about the scripture, "Be wise in the way you act toward outsiders; make the most of every opportunity" (Col. 4:5 NIV). We talked several more times and he allowed me to pray with him. He and his family were moving the next week, but he promised they would find a good church and he would give it more than one try even if he didn't like the music or he thought they talked about money too much. I know this scenario did not just happen. God orchestrates our lives as we surrender to Him moment by moment.

The New Living Translation of Psalm 37:5 says it this way: "The Lord directs the steps of the godly. He delights in every detail of their life."

God was providing for me and giving me wisdom for all these decisions and I did give thanks but still had those awful lonely times at night. My friend, Amy had more major decisions than I when her husband Brad died of cancer at the age of fifty-seven. After many years of music ministry and teaching, they were finally getting on their feet financially. Five years earlier, Brad had suffered from a tumor on his kidney but was given a clean bill of health. They decided to cash in their whole life policy to build a home for retirement. When they took out a term life insurance, the company did not express any concern about the previous kidney tumor; however, when Amy tried to cash in the policy, they would not pay. This meant Amy had to go right back to work to a position of great responsibility. Having time for the grief process was put on hold.

During this time, she felt so alone and even abandoned as her one daughter and family made a move to another community and her other daughter, a single mom, moved in with her. Of course, they were a comfort to each other, but Amy needed to grieve. After her daughter moved, she realized she needed to do something different. Should she sell her home? Brad had built it for her retirement. She told God that she needed some definite directives from sources other than her church where she was on staff. They came.

The first was her realtor from a previous sale of their condo, who called one day and just casually mentioned that if she ever thought about selling, now would be the time to do it. Next, Amy's psychologist sister called to suggest that perhaps Amy had put her "grieving on hold" due to family issues and ministry. She must deal with it now. Third, Amy visited her doctor for an unrelated issue. While talking, she had a complete meltdown which is completely out of character for her. Her doctor told her that she needed to make changes.

Amy called the realtor, put the house on the market at noon and had three showings and three offers that day...above the asking price. Seems that Brad did finish their home for her retirement. Her next decision was to take an early retirement from the church where she had ministered for fifteen years. God has blessed her with a wonderful place to live and provided her husband's full social security disability. Once all this happened, she felt a great burden lifted. As she was telling me this, I began to weep as I visualized God's loving arms outstretched to take care of another one of his widowed daughters. We may not always see how things are going to work, but we know Who is in charge. I have this verse on a three-by-five card and placed in several places in my home. I say it over and over. "He (God) is before all things, and in him, all things hold together" (Col. 1:17 NIV).

If you are a widow, please know that God is there for you through all the ups and downs. I've never struggled with making decisions so was surprised how challenging it was during those first two years. While sitting in the hospital when Doug was ill, I was impressed to memorize Isaiah 40:29–31 (NIV).

> Do you not know? Have you not heard? The Lord is the everlasting God, the creator of the ends of the earth. He will not grow tired or weary and His understanding no one can fathom. He gives strength to the weary and increases the power of the weak. Even youth grow tired and weary and young men stumble and fall, but those who wait on the Lord will mount up with wings like eagles. They will run and not be weary. They will walk and not faint.

I would pray these words and say, "Oh, Lord, I am weary and tired. Thank you for not being weary. I don't understand your plan, but I know from your creation, that you are holding all things together. Thank you for always being there. Help me to rely on these promises as I wait."

Lori and Rod were looking forward to an early retirement. He had worked sixty and seventy hours per week as a computer technician while she stayed on the home front taking care of their children as well as running a day care in their home. After the children were grown, she became a master gardener as he continued to work long hours. Now they would be able to travel…maybe even purchase a motor home. Within a few months of his retirement, he became ill and was eventually diagnosed with cancer. They had moved to the other side of the state to be closer to family so were missing their former church family and friends. Many trips to the University of Michigan hospital for testing and later hospitalization took place over a two-year period.

Lori was not only devastated from losing the love of her life. She lost her financial planner and decision maker. Unfortunately, Rod did not show her the budget or how to pay the bills. She simply trusted his words "You don't need to worry." In the last months, she would call me and ask what she should do since he did not even have a will. I advised her to work with the hospital staff who finally convinced him to sign the needed papers. Rod did really love Lori and was good to her. They had been high school sweethearts, but he was in that generation where the husband protected the wife by "handling things." He had recommitted his life to God in the previous five years, but still had that mindset. Amazingly, Lori has done a great job "handling" things. During the seven months that he has been gone, she has sold many of his expensive toys, prepared taxes, finished remodeling on the house and taken care of all financial obligations. Turned out to be a good thing that her name was not on the credit cards. God truly does work for the good of those who love Him and are called according to His purpose (Rom. 8:26).

Whether home repair, selling homes, purchasing cars, or investing, widows struggle in different ways. Some of us have family members to help us and some have family members who hinder like Lori. Her in-laws actually claimed the home belonged to them. Later, her own children urged her to sell the home and come live with them. They refused to help her as she completely remodeled and still after two years have not come for a visit. She has some sad days, but keeps her head high and still goes to visit them. How can she do that? Only by the grace of God.

While Mary was having her kitchen remodeled, she witnessed to every worker who came in as to God's grace and strength to live as a widow. One story she told was when she and her family got ready to go on vacation, she could not find the little black bag that Jack always stored cash in for their vacations. It was not in the bureau drawer where he always kept it. She and her family thought maybe Jack had laid it down when they were Christmas shopping. They asked God to help them find it, but if not, they hoped whoever found it would use it wisely and be blessed. They decided to go anyway. When she opened one of the suitcases to pack, the little black bag appeared. God often surprises us with his provision.

Kim waited a year to sell her huge home in the country and then bought a condo down the street from me. She tells everyone that I found her condo at a garage sale. She had mentioned to me that she was looking so when I saw a garage sale there, I asked if the condo was for sale. They said, "Not yet, but it will be." Eventually, all the transactions took place without a realtor. Through all of this, God's grace just kept showing up. It will do the same for you as you move forward on your journey.

Helps for Making Financial and Other Major Decisions

1. Find all Social Security papers as needed and your marriage license. Either make an appointment or arrive early on a Wednesday at the office.
2. If you cannot find all of the needed documents, the agents there will help you. If you have a difficult time communicating with one agent, ask for another.
3. Call your life insurance company for directives. If you have a sizable amount, place it in the bank in your name until you can make a decision about investments.
4. If you do not already have a financial advisor, ask your pastor or another strong Christian for advice.
5. Make a list of bills you need to pay. If your husband paid all of the bills and died suddenly, seek help from the financial advisor, a trusted friend, or research from books in the bibliography of this book.
6. Unless really needed, don't purchase new furniture or other major appliances within the first year.
7. If a tombstone is needed, your funeral director will help you. I found private establishments more expensive.
8. If your loved one died in the hospital, you may not be liable for certain bills. If you are, the hospital should work with you on a noninterest payment plan.
9. If credit cards are in your husband's name, you should not be responsible.
10. Don't take your husband's name off joint banking accounts for at least six months in case certain checks for rebates or rewards might be directly deposited.

11. Your trusted banker should be able to give you advise when to put all accounts in your name only. He will also advise you about beneficiaries.
12. Put cars, home, and other major belongings in your name only for tax purposes.
13. Update your will or see a lawyer about writing one.
14. Keep all tax papers together.
15. Google is a wonderful tool. Your local library has wonderful books especially on grieving. I have listed several of those in my bibliography.
16. Above all, don't try to do everything in a short period. Choose the most important and do one or two per day. Ask for God's continual wisdom and comfort and "Don't forget to thank him" (Phil. 4:6b NLT).

4

Handling Those "Firsts"

Doug passed away in February with his birthday to have been the next month. Since two of my adult children and one grandchild also have March birthdays, we always had a big party for everyone. I struggled to keep the tradition alive as I prepared all their favorite foods, decorated the house, and wrapped gifts. I even invited my daughter-in-law's parents. We did have a good time as we laughed and talked about things Doug would have done and said if he had been there. There were times of crying as my oldest son expressed his anger as to why his dad had to leave us when he had seemed so young and vibrant and helpful to others. We all talked about Doug's greatest gifts to us and rejoiced for the years we did have and that he would not suffer any more.

After everyone left, I felt so empty. My children wanted to comfort me, but I felt that I needed to comfort them. I wanted them to help more, have more ideas on ways to celebrate and even to help more with set up and clean up. I'm pretty sure my grief intensified my feelings of frustration. I knew I should have been giving thanks, but did not feel like it. So glad I pushed on through to victory as I remembered 1 Thessalonians 5:17, which says, "Be joyful always, pray continually; give thanks in all circumstances." As I read, I cried out, "But God, how can I be joyful when I've just lost the love of my life? I am praying continually, but it seems to be more of a 'Help,

I'm drowning' type prayer. How can I give thanks?" Each time, God answered in that still small voice within. "You can be joyful because you are my child and you had all those great years with a godly man. You can be joyful because your children love to come to your home. You can be joyful because you have my promise of "I will never leave you or forsake you" (Heb. 13:5b NIV).

On April 1 (no fooling), I experienced some chest pain and was rushed to the hospital for an angiogram, which showed a need for stents. I couldn't believe it. I walked two to three miles every day, went to the gym, participated in line dancing classes, ate pretty healthy, and no one in my family had ever suffered from heart problems. (All that really paid off in my short time of healing.) Once again, God's strength showed up as I went alone to cardiac rehab three days per week. Even there, God helped me to remain positive and try to encourage others. One lady, who also lived alone, always looked so sad. I began to pray that I could encourage her, but there never seemed to be a time when it was appropriate to talk to her. One day, she and I "just happened" to be the only two in the locker room. She poured out her heart to me, and I was able to show her the comfort God had given me. The Apostle Paul expresses this so beautifully in 2 Corinthians 1:3. "Praise be to the God and Father of our Lord Jesus Christ, the Father of compassion and the God of all comfort."

Easter came two weeks after I had the heart procedure, and I didn't have the energy for our usual celebration. I sat on the front row as my pastor son baptized about twenty people while I sat with his young son. Looking back to that time helps me to realize how great God's grace was that I was able to rejoice and enjoy my family. How could I not when Jesus suffered so much more than I ever could? Then He rose again just as the people being baptized, but he sent his Holy Spirit to be with me, to comfort me and to give me wisdom. Even as I write today, my heart swells with thankfulness for His great love. He has kept me, is keeping me, and will continue to hold me and my family in the palm of His hand. Many times when I've felt like I was slipping through his fingers, he has tightened his grip. I often quote Psalm 18:1–2: "I love you Lord, my strength. The Lord is my rock, my refuge, and my deliverer. My God is my rock in whom I take refuge, my shield, the horn of my salvation, my stronghold. I look to the Lord who is worthy of praise."

Doug always planned a special getaway for my birthday such as a trip to a nearby resort or just a special dinner with friends. We usually went shopping together to choose a piece of jewelry or an outfit. What a blessed lady I was that he liked to watch me model different outfits so he could tell me which looked the best. Now that he was gone, how would I spend my birthday? My youngest son invited me to go with him to Florida on one of his business trips. Since he was in charge of the workshops, he was able to arrange his schedule to take me to dinner each evening and he gave me an iPad Mini as a very special birthday gift. Even though I was thankful for my son's generosity, I felt so alone as I sat by the pool. Yes, there were people there, happy couples and children, but I felt alone. About the time, I was ready to pick up my towel and go back to my room, my handsome son walked around the corner. I began to replace my sadness with thanks. Now, this is easier said than done. As I silently cried out for God's help, the words of Psalm 16:8 (NASB) came to my mind. "I have set the Lord continuously before me; because He is at my right hand, I will not be shaken." As my son left, I began to watch the children at the pool and have great memories about Doug's and my times with our boys.

On my next birthday, I planned a little excursion to the beach, our favorite place. Having moved to Michigan in the early nineties, we spent many days at various Lake Michigan beaches. Although, it's hard for a widow to return to places where she shared so much love and fun with her husband, the crystal-clear water and soothing waves brought great healing. Afterward, I went to a jewelry store and chose a ring that I cherish as if it were from him. I don't do that for every birthday now, but that second year, it somehow brought me comfort. I read all the cards from him on previous birthdays, cried and cried, and rejoiced for such a love. In recent years, when birthdays come around, I surround myself with fun activities and flowers especially roses. They were Doug's favorite. "The Lord is my strength and my song; he has become my salvation (Ps. 118:14).

My children tried to make one of my birthdays very special by having my youngest son fly in from Pennsylvania as a surprise. My birthday was actually on a Sunday. Much to my disapproval, my pastor son was having the congregation sing "Happy Birthday" to me as I looked up to see my youngest son slide next to me in the row where I was sitting. The next day, they planned a brunch with gifts and cake. Since I was the one who always planned all the parties, they kept asking me about things like, "Who brought the syrup?" or "Where is the fruit?" I actually had to start the cooking because no one knew where to begin. (I'm sure I taught them.) My one daughter-in-law tried to keep things rolling as we all laughed and just worked together. At first, I was a little hurt that they didn't plan things better but realized they were really trying. They were grieving too and learning how to live as a family without their precious dad. Again, God helped me to give thanks that I had children who loved me rather than fretting over how things were done. He often reminded me in those early days of grief that I was especially sensitive due to my grief. I'm so thankful for the book I read years ago by Evelyn Christianson entitled *Lord Change Me*. Yes, I knew I was the one who must change. That's how the Holy Spirit works by bringing to our memory those things that will help us.

On one occasion, my family kept asking me what I wanted to do for my birthday. I'm thinking, *Don't you know I can't think of what I want. I just want you to plan it.* I had suggested a certain restaurant for breakfast, but they forgot to tell me about a special school event they went to. At first, I was so hurt, but as I prayed, I remembered that Doug went out to breakfast by himself often when I was teaching and had to be at the middle school by 7:30 a.m. I called on God for strength, thought about the sausage and biscuits, and went (yes, all by myself) to the restaurant. As I looked around, I saw several people eating alone, either reading the newspaper or checking emails on their phones. *This is not so bad*, I thought as I ordered my favorite. I still felt a little out of sorts but was proud that I stepped out to do this. I was "out of my comfort zone," but God was there with me.

Eating alone even at home can also be daunting. First of all, it might be a challenge just to come up with a menu plan. Then it's hard to cook for just one. Nina's husband died a few years before mine, and later she told me that Sundays were so hard. She would often stop by the grocery store, pick up a rotisserie chicken to take home, and eat alone. How sad! Why did I not know this? We could have had her eat with us. She graciously accepted my apology, and we began talking about all the things you can do with one rotisserie chicken; just as a meal with a salad, make soup, chicken enchiladas or quesadillas, chicken pot pie, a chicken sandwich, or chicken pot pie. We even talked about writing a cookbook entitled *Single Again, What's the Menu Plan?* We agreed that planning meal times when our favorite TV shows were on or scrolling through Facebook or emails kept us from feeling alone. Sometimes my adult children FaceTime me at dinner. Another idea might be to take turns cooking with another single person.

That afternoon of my birthday, my daughter-in-law asked again what I wanted to do so I tried to be helpful and suggested a picnic at a nearby lake beach. She was great with that and talked about what food we should have. Again, I was disappointed that I brought the main course and they forgot several essential items needed for a picnic such as plates and napkins. This sounds like a grumpy and ungrateful person, or maybe someone who is in deep grief and is not capable of making decisions. Several birthdays have come and gone since then where this family has been marvelous with boat rides, special gifts, and expeditions that I love. I realize now that they were also grieving that Dad was not there to keep the party going. They did not and could not understand my grief, nor could I understand theirs. Once again, I had to let them off the hook of my expectations.

Our wedding anniversary never came at a good time. It was that time of the year when I was getting my classroom ready for the new year and, of course, school clothes for the boys. Always supportive of my teaching, Doug tried to keep things simple, yet meaningful. One time, when we had just moved and I had not secured a teaching job yet, he planned a trip to Niagara Falls. The online description of our place indicated that it was within walking distance from the falls, so we took off after dinner. We walked and walked and walked. By the time we got back to the hotel, we were so exhausted that Doug fell asleep in the recliner within minutes. On our fortieth anniversary, we took a trip to the Bahamas, never thinking that August is so hot there. Every day was above 110 degrees. We could not go out during the middle of the day and discovered why most people choose the "all-inclusive" trips. Oh well! Great memories.

Every widow probably has a different holiday or special day that is the hardest for her. Mine is definitely the anniversary. Doug always chose such beautiful cards with just the right words, but I didn't usually read those first. I read what he wrote at the bottom. From being a struggling writer as a college freshman, he became prolific and poetic. In the last few years, he would say something like, "This has been a challenging year, but we can face any challenge as long as we have each other. Surely our future will only get better." It did not, but our love grew deeper. On what would have been our fiftieth, I was especially sad as I sat on the beach thinking about all that we could be doing. I asked the Lord to help me change my thoughts toward gratitude. Immediately, I began to write fifty things I missed most about Doug…things for which to give thanks. This great therapy kept me from spiraling down into depression. I've included some of them here to perhaps guide other widows in a similar exercise.

1. His smile and the way his eyes lit up when I came into the room
2. The dimple in his left cheek
3. His smooth base voice—talking and singing
4. His watching me cook and making sure to turn on the light above the stove
5. Always telling me how cute I was and helping me shop
6. Grabbing my hand while riding in the car or sitting on the couch
7. Asking me how I could love him so much
8. Watching him play cars or fish with the grandsons
9. Listening to my teacher stories and telling me how blessed they made him feel
10. Praying for me

11. His corny jokes and dry sense of humor, mischievous grin, and whistle
12. Keeping things repaired around the house
13. Sitting on the beach reading a good book and interrupting me to tell me what it said
14. Riding bikes together
15. Coming up behind me in the kitchen, kissing me on the neck
16. His walk up to the platform to preach on Sundays
17. His "everything will be all right" demeanor
18. Coming home to find him snoozing on the couch...he loved power naps.
19. Showing him my great bargains from shopping trips with the girls
20. Praying together for our sons and their families

When I read the psalmist David's words in Psalm 103, I know he is talking about much deeper things, but it helps me to realize that one of God's greatest benefits is the grace He shows in "redeeming my life from the pit" (Ps. 103:4a NIV).

That first Thanksgiving found our family participating in our usual tradition of each giving thanks for the highlight of our year. Since my oldest son dropped the turkey as he was pulling it out of the oven, my youngest who has a sense of humor like his dad's gave thanks that the turkey was still all in one piece or should I say, "Bird"? Like his dad, he always wanted the whole turkey displayed for a family picture. Laughing is a good thing on the journey of grief. As we bowed our head to pray, I suddenly remembered that I was now the head of the home and needed to ask my oldest son to pray for the meal and our family. After we ate, each person gave thanks for a memory of Papa as well as the one thing from the past year for which they were most thankful. I can't remember all of them, but I do remember the tears and laughter...all a necessary part of healing. Tears are surely a language God understands.

With a pastor son and one who is on staff at a large church in Ohio, planning a time for everyone to get together for the holidays seems next to impossible. Of course my children have always been accustomed to my doing the planning. I should have been so much stronger. After all, it had been ten months since Doug's passing. I was but not strong enough. By this time, I was able to tell them I needed help and to delegate. My sons tried to do some of the things their dad had done such as read the Christmas story from Luke. My middle son was doing a great job when suddenly, he broke down in tears. Tears are good. We needed to grieve and then rejoice at new life through Christ. That second Christmas without Papa also brought us a new grandson who is the image of his papa...even to the dimple in the cheek and the big blue eyes. More laughter and tears...a great combo.

Lori expressed her deep sadness because her children refuse to come to her home. They always want her to come to theirs. This was her first Christmas without Rod and she struggled to be in her daughter's home without him. Everyone was laughing, opening gifts, and eating. Then came the time for her to go to her room alone... no one to cuddle with or talk about the day. I was able to share with her that her children were probably not ready to go into the home where their dad was so ill. It has been two years now since his passing and they still do not come even though they live only an hour away. When I called her last week, she was weeping over the hurt she felt and asked me what she should do. I was able to share from the book *Healing the Adult Child's Grieving Heart* by Alan D. Wolfelt, PhD. He explains how some adult children are saying they are doing well, which might be interpreted as "They are avoiding their pain." He goes on to say that some people can only let pain into their lives in small doses.

On our third Christmas without Doug, we had all celebrated early due to my son's church responsibilities. Since the weather was actually nice in northern Ohio on Lake Erie, my middle son asked if I wanted to spend the next week at their home. As can often happen, things became tense between the teens and their parents. I felt like the buffer and had no one with whom to debrief. The guys were arguing about losing their wallets and of course the parents were upset. When the younger boy came down to the living room where

I was pretending to read, I asked him if he had prayed about finding the wallet. We did, and I felt impressed to have him look in a place where he had already looked. You guessed it! God came through and there it was back in a dark corner of the desk. God seemed to be whispering in my ear, "You are needed here."

I continued to struggle being in their home without Doug. I remember healing taking place one night as the older grandsons and I were playing games. Since there are two of them, we could not do teams as they often did with their mom's parents. I told them I was sorry that I did not have a papa for them. The older grandson exclaimed, "Gramma, we love having you here even without Papa. We don't ever want a new papa." I realized that I did feel very loved and comfortable. It's one of those "aha" moments in the journey of grief. I really am making progress. God's love and comfort and surround me. "As the mountains surround Jerusalem so the Lord surrounds His people" (Ps. 125:2 NIV).

Mary, who lost her husband two days after Christmas, shared that she really needed her adult children and their families to be in her home. Both her children wanted her to come to their homes which actually seems reasonable because all the children and gifts were there. Widows cannot expect their adult children to understand. They actually thought they were making it easier for her. Christmas had always been at Gramma and PopPop's house with both families. Now she could not plan and decorate as usual. Traditions were being torn down. I think I might be the only one she told about not wanting to drive in the winter weather and how sad she was to not have everyone at her home like always. Three Christmases have come and gone since then. She still decorates her house as if they were coming but goes an hour north to her daughter's home. Someday she might be able to express her feelings to them, but being the loving and deeply spiritual mom and grandma that she is, her only response is thankfulness. Our lives and our traditions continue to change as God's grace and comfort grow more abundant. "The Lord is gracious and righteous. Our God is full of compassion. The Lord protects the simplehearted. When I was in great need, He saved me. Be at rest, O my soul for the Lord has been good to you" (Ps. 116:5–7 NIV).

Being the wonderful cook and hostess that she is, Teresa invited all the children and families to her home that first Christmas, five months after Rick's death. One problem! They wanted to tell her what to cook and how to arrange everything. Guess they didn't think about the fact that their dad had not been the one to do the planning in previous years. Siblings were arguing over who got what memoirs, and they were upset that Mom threw some things away...private journals of her husband. They even suggested that she was spending too much money when they really did not even know how well their dad had provided for her. Teresa realized they had her best interest at heart but eventually had to tell them that she would make those decisions and they could put their minds to rest about her care.

When talking to my widow friends and acquaintances, I find that the anniversary date of their loved one's passing is often the hardest. On the first-year anniversary, I found roses on my front porch with a note of love from one of my sons. All of them usually put something on Facebook like a tribute to their dad and their thankfulness for our wonderful marriage. The sixth year was the first that two of them did not call or text. That's okay. I'm stronger now, and I know they are busy with their own families. The second year, I was reading from Sarah Young's *Jesus Calling* devotional book. Right there on that page, the exact date that he passed, was his favorite verse. "If anyone is in Christ, he is a new creation; the old is gone. The new has come" (2 Cor. 5:17 NIV). The Holy Spirit's Awareness flooded my soul as I gave thanks for those words on that particular day. It almost seemed like God knew February 17 was the day Doug would pass and He directed Sarah Young to use that scripture for her devotional.

Valentine's Day was an especially rough day for me since Doug always remembered it more than other holidays. Birthdays and anniversaries sometimes needed a little prompting such as "Oh, look, Doug, that would make a great birthday gift for me." No problem with Valentine's Day, not only because Doug loved chocolate too, but because he loved me so much. Doug was in the hospital on our last Valentine's Day together. Even though he was in pain and feeling quite weak, he continued to have a great sense of humor. When our sons came into the room as I was bathing him, they ask why I didn't just have the nurse do the bath. Doug turned to them with that glint in his big blue eyes and said, "Now, guys, it *is* Valentine's Day." Every Valentine's Day since his passing, I have found roses or other flower arrangements on my front porch from one of the sons. I read cards from previous years. I don't buy chocolate, even though I love it. Well, maybe just a little piece for special occasions.

Gayle reports that Easter was hard for her because she and her late husband had been a big part of the large pageant presented every year. Her husband had built many of the props, and she was to have sung a solo. Amy says June is so hard for her because it was the month of his birthday, their anniversary, and Father's Day. She tries to overcome by celebrating with her two sons-in-law. Teresa reports feeling so sad when none of her children remembered her birthday except for one text.

A few years after Doug's passing, I noticed that I didn't have many pictures taken on those special days. I realized that I always handed off chores or babies to Doug so I could take the pictures. I've had to learn to delegate more and even have my oldest grandson take pictures. The widow must develop strategies for keeping positive. When everyone leaves and there are still dishes in the sink, she turns on the music and dances through the chores. She looks at the picture of her sweetheart on the mantle and says, "Good night, sweetheart. I surely miss you and your help, but am learning to delegate and enjoy life again. Your life will continue to change. You will develop new traditions, go new and different places, eat foods you like that your spouse did not care for, and watch movies that you choose. Healing sometimes comes slowly but we keep walking as the lepers in Luke 17:11–19. Jesus told them to go show themselves. They could not see any physical healing, but obeyed. "And as they went, they were cleansed" (Luke 17:14b NIV). We, too, will experience healing as we keep walking.

Suggestions For Handling the Special "Firsts"

1. Plan a fun activity such as lunch or a movie with a friend. Better yet, visit a friend in a warmer place.
2. Read through old cards from your loved one.
3. Purchase his favorite flowers and cake. Share it with a neighbor or friend.
4. On your birthday, etc., purchase a gift for yourself that he might have chosen.
5. Make a list of all your blessings including great memories.
6. Write in your journal...even the sad thoughts. You will begin to see progress over the years.
7. Thank your adult children for ways they bless you.
8. Spend time listening to great music.
9. Go to the gym or for a walk knowing that your loved one would be so proud of you.
10. Make a list of other widow's birthdays, anniversaries, and dates of their husband's passing. Call them or send a card. Always pray for them as you remember that many of them are praying for you.

5

Going Places Alone

Whether it is facing going into the bedroom at night and knowing there is no one with whom to cuddle or going out to a restaurant to eat alone, most widows struggle. I've never slept alone. Even when a child, I had to sleep with a sibling since there were six of us…seemed my sister always had her foot on my side of the bed. Finally, when married, I found a great sleeping partner. Going to sleep without each other was always difficult. Right after Doug passed, I was so exhausted that I slept great even with a house full of people. I was so thankful for all their help, but was ready to be alone… I thought. As I walked into the bedroom that night and saw those pillows where he had lain, my heart plunged to my stomach as I threw myself across the bed and wept with abandonment. Within a few months, I changed the bed coverings and snuggled up against his pillows. I kept three-by-five cards on my bedside table with scripture verses. When I couldn't sleep or remember God's promises, I would read and pray those promises over and over. A few years before Doug passed, the Holy Spirit impressed me to memorize Psalm 63:1–8 (NIV). I didn't know why, but I worked diligently and for at least three months to do so. This is especially amazing since I haven't been able to memorize such a long passage since. As you read these words, you can see how helpful they were to me as I awoke during the night or couldn't even get to sleep. Even after all these years, I never forget these words.

> Oh, God, you are my God. Earnestly, I seek you. My soul thirsts for you. My body longs for you in a dry and thirsty land where there is no water. I have seen you in your sanctuary and beheld your power and glory. Because your love is better than life, my lips will praise you. I will praise you as long as I live, and in your name, I will lift my hands. My soul will be satisfied as with the richest of foods. With singing lips, my mouth will praise you. On my bed, I remember you. I think of you through the watches of the night. Because you are my help, I sing in the shadow of your wings. My soul clings to you. Your right hand upholds me.

Most of the widows with whom I've talked, struggle with getting back into a regular sleep pattern or even being able to sleep. I've never been a great sleeper so was not overly concerned. When a widow has young children or she has to go back to work, the concern is greater. In my case, I would just get up and wander around the house, read my scripture cards, or turn on the fireplace and listen to music. I would have sought help from my doctor if I could not have functioned the next day. Paula D'Arcy in her book *When People Grieve* writes, "Grief calls us to slow down and allow the sadness to pass through so a deep-rootedness may be found." She goes on to say that it is time to seek professional help if "there are no breaks between the darkest throws of pain."

The widow not only loses her soul mate. She loses her chauffer, the accountant, home repairman, yard man, car maintenance guy, last-minute errand runner, plumber, food taster, and travel companion. On one occasion, when my family with four boys was visiting, I was feeling especially in need of Doug's help as I cleaned and cooked and made time for playing with the toddlers. My thirteen-year-old grandson had an interesting question. "Gramma, you probably have a lot more time now that Papa has gone to heaven."

For some reason, I was calm enough to ask, "What makes you say that?"

"Well, you only have half as much laundry and half as much food to cook and trash to take out." I patiently (on the outside anyway) explained to him that Papa took all the trash out, always emptied the dishwasher, and that I still had the same number of pans. Papa also took care of all the car needs, paid the bills, and did all the home repairs. I could see the wheels turning in his head as he asked, "Wow! I never thought of that. Do you need some help? I could clean your car." Since that time, I've noticed that people often think a single person has more time when quite the opposite is true. We have a choice. We can either be willing to be misunderstood or stay frustrated.

For years, we went on vacation to a beach with our best friends and their children. Once the children left home, we couples continued to go. We girls loved to plan menus and organize events. When October came the year after Doug passed, I was still involved in making decisions about home remodeling and going to a grief share group. My vacation friends came to my condo and helped, creating a mini vacation right there as we girls prepared fun dinners and we all played games in the evening. We began to talk about my going with them to the beach the next year. They suggested that I invite one of my widow friends. Since I had two close ones, I invited both. We singles girls decided to drive down in my car and meet the couples there.

My emotional state was fragile, not only from this being the same place where Doug and I had gone, but because my aunt, who was like a mom to me, was quite ill. The doctors had even called in the family. On the way to our condo, I suggested that if she did pass away, I would fly from South Carolina to Texas to be with family. One of the girls felt uneasy about my leaving her with people she did not know so well. The whole week was a little tense with my trying to please everyone. I wanted to visit with my couple friends while at the same time making my lady friends feel comfortable. My aunt did pass away, but I did not go to the funeral even though I would have been gone for only two days. I'm still not sure I made the right decision, but God brought me comfort as I wrote a letter of tribute to my cousins about their amazing mom.

The next year, I told my couple friends that I would not be going. I felt so loved as they told me that we were family and just because Doug died, they still wanted me. Then they really laid the guilt on as they tried to assure me that Doug would have gone if I had died first. I'm not so sure about that, but I told them I would give it a try. I rode with one couple on the way there and the other on the way back. We were all having a great time as we met for lunch and arrived at our halfway point, a hotel in North Carolina. It seemed strange that we were having dinner with an empty place in the booth beside me, but I was okay...at least until it came time for me to go to my room. Gracious! They were just down the hall and I had been sleeping alone for two years. Grief reared its ugly head again. I cried out to the Lord and He gave me the impression that I could either lie there and cry or I could praise God for my wonderful friends and look forward to the trip. Two miles on the treadmill in the workout room as I praised God for His blessings did the trick. Please don't think this was easy. I think I spent the first three years of my grief journey saying, "Help, Lord. I need direction to climb out of this horrible pit. God surely does continually "redeem our lives from the pit" (Ps. 103:4a).

My friends worked so hard to make me feel comfortable as we played games...trying to never have games that required partners. I felt comfortable telling them that I rejoiced in their love and wanted them to relax, hold hands, and sneak in those little kisses as Doug and I had always done and would be doing if he were there. I did struggle when we were playing miniature golf and they would walk hand in hand to the next hole. By the third vacation, I had made friends with a wonderful younger widow who wanted to go with us. Finally, a perfect match. She and I loved to just sit on the beach and read a good book or go walking. The couples liked visiting museums and other attractions during the day. At night we would have dinner, Bible study, and play games. Again, the grieving process takes time and work. So glad I did not give up on my vacations with my couple friends. Mostly, I'm glad for God's comfort and wisdom to face every situation. He assures me with his word, "Forget the former things; do not dwell on the past. See, I am doing a new thing. Now, it springs up" (Isa. 43:18).

Mary and her family always rented a house on the ocean each July. The first year after Jack died, she planned every detail. Her five grandchildren were so excited. Only one problem...there was a big hole with her husband and their papa not there. The kids all did their best to make her feel loved, but she had to deal with going to bed alone, making most of the arrangements, having no one with whom to debrief when the grandchildren had arguments or she felt left out of certain activities. About a week after the trip, I felt impressed to call. Struggling to talk through her tears, she expressed her heart-ache and despair. We cried together knowing that next year would be better. I'm so thankful for encouragement from others and God's leading me to share as the Apostle Paul tells us in 1 Corinthians 1:4 that we serve the God of all comfort. "Who comforts us in all our troubles, so that we can comfort those in any trouble with the comfort we ourselves receive from God" (2 Cor. 1:4).

In June after Doug's passing in February, a season of graduation parties and weddings commenced. One of the first was a family who had been members of our last pastorate. Since they lived on a lake, I was escorted via golf cart down to their lovely home. Looking over the sea of faces already seated, I wondered where I should sit as a single person. Everyone was really friendly, but no one invited me to come to their table. As I was standing there, the older brother of the graduate came to offer his condolences. He then began telling me a story about how Doug had helped him as a teen. His words, "I was at a church picnic when Pastor Doug came up to ask me how sports and school were going. I told him about my discouragement in writ-ing. He told me that he had really struggled too and when he went to college, his teacher told him that his writing was like that of a sixth grader. Low blow! He began to pray and God led him to a wonderful girl who was a pretty good reader and writer. She taught him some basic principles of writing and he just kept at it and prayed for God to give him wisdom. He did and his grades went from Ds to As."

Brandon was inspired to get some help and is now a journalist for an overseas news station. I'm so glad I went to the party. I was hearing how Doug's ministry was continuing. Every party I went to was the same. What a boost to my mood. How wonderful to know Doug's influence is still alive. Once again, I'm thankful God helped me to plow through my feelings of insecurity and take the risk to attend a function alone.

Graduations were one thing. Weddings brought even more discomfort. I was thankful to be invited to our former associate's daughter's wedding. She had also been one of my second-grade students. I understand why the seating was not arranged for me to sit with another single person, but it was really hard to sit next to the empty chair. All was beautiful, and then it was time for dancing. Watching the happy couples brought tears that I could not hide so I quietly left when the dancing began. Just two years later, I went to another wedding to which my son and family were also invited. We had so much fun. The groom had a young single friend there who wanted to know if I could be his "date." We laughed and I was able to share my faith with him. Over the years, I've been invited to fewer and fewer of our former church members' weddings. I have mixed feelings. On one side, I am thinking, "If Doug were here, we would be invited and attending. On the other hand, I really don't want to go alone...just another adjustment, but more and more minor as the years go by." After eight years, it is now time for my own grandsons to be graduating and getting married. I'm thrilled that I will be there...even alone.

My high school reunion was planned for the fall in the year Doug passed away. It would have been our first time to go since Texas was so far away, and we were always working or ministering. I had decided not to go alone until my youngest son asked if he could go and even offered to pay for everything. He wanted to see my hometown and meet some of my school friends. Walking in unnoticed was not possible as one of my beautiful friends and the former homecoming queen stood up and exclaimed loudly, "Look, guys, it's Paula. She has finally been able to come." We had a great time at the dinner and evening events. The next day, my son wanted to drive all over town and see the places my family and I had lived when I was growing up and the church that had been so instrumental in nurturing me. As we sat in my former next-door neighbor's home that afternoon, she began to describe to my son how I was the one who had invited her to church and that she wondered where she would be now if her life had not been committed to Christ. I did not remember those times, but was so thankful to hear the words, see her life, and for my son to hear. God's grace is truly amazing

The next morning, my son had to fly out earlier than I. There I was in this huge luxurious hotel on the twelfth floor surrounded by glass windows that made me feel like I was in heaven. Suddenly, I awoke in a state of panic as I thought, *No one knows where I am. Who would I call in this huge city of Dallas if something went wrong? After all, I had just had a heart event right after Doug died. What if I lost my ticket or missed the bus to the airport?* I fell to my knees and asked for God's peace and protection. As I finally drifted off to sleep, I dreamed that Doug was standing in the clouds with his arms outstretched. I went to him, and as he put his arms around me, I begged him to take me with him. I heard his calm and mellow voice saying, "Not now, Paula." When I awoke, I had a great sense of calm, got ready, and made it to my van on time. That sense of calmness and the sound of his voice and the feel of his arms stayed with me all the way back to Michigan. The peace that God gives is so different from the world's. John 14:27 expresses it this way in the Living Bible: "And the peace I give isn't fragile like the world gives. So don't be troubled or afraid."

Several of my pastor's wives widow friends have indicated that Sundays are their most difficult days. They are no longer the pastor's wife...in some cases, worship leader or musician. They expressed their sadness at not seeing their spouse in the pulpit. We all have different reactions, and I am thankful that I felt the most comfortable at church on Sunday mornings. I would visualize Doug worshiping around the throne. That surely doesn't make me any more spiritual. Sunday afternoons were the worst for me. The day would seem so long with no one to debrief with or go to dinner with. Sometimes, my son and family would invite me, but they had so many ministries to attend. I could not bring myself to invite others at this point. Two years later, I began to invite other singles to lunch, but the day still seemed long and lonely, especially on days with dreary, rainy weather. One day, as I was telling God about my feelings, he reminded me that I had lonely days sometimes even when Doug was alive. He was not nearly as social as I, so many times when others were enjoying social events, we were at home. Just as I adjusted to that, I knew God would help me to adjust by finding different things to keep my interest. My thinking actually went from "I am so lonely" to "I can go anywhere I want. I can watch any show I want, eat anything I want. Being single is not all bad." I know that was God getting me "unstuck from my grief." I love the way author Sheila Walsch in her book *It's Okay Not to Be Okay* explains that we need to "move into a new way of thinking." She goes on to say, "We place more emphasis on behavior rather than on right thinking—on what we do rather than why we do it."

Doing all the driving and finding places all by myself has become an adventure. So thankful for GPS! In spring of the first year of Doug's passing, I decided to drive to Philadelphia, Pennsylvania, to visit my youngest son. On the way, I would stop at my middle son's home in Cleveland and get to visit with my three grandsons. It was a long...trip, even though I had great music and books on CD. Arriving at 4:00 p.m. in the big city was not a good thing with bumper-to-bumper traffic in the downtown area where he lived. I walked in and plopped my bags on the counter and declared, "I've learned a lot on this trip and the main thing is that I will never drive that far by myself again." I did feel a sense of accomplishment but realized I didn't need to accomplish that again. I'm sure it made me a better driver because one of my sweet friends calmly mentioned one day that I was a much better driver now. I smiled to myself as I thought about the many times I had probably scared her.

Doing all the grocery shopping, and putting everything away was something we did together after Doug retired. Even before then, he helped to carry everything in and put it away. I loved our Friday night dates as he called our late-night trips to the store. Little treats that were not on the list were often found in the basket at check out. Of course, I have fewer groceries now but still a considerable amount as one of my gifts is hospitality and cooking for people who are experiencing losses in their lives. Having people over for dinner without a spouse has been quite the feat. Even though my family helps, I often find that I'm still putting things away late that night because I am too tired while the families are there. I found it to be exhausting to make sure everyone was served, talked with, and their needs met. After seven years, I am much more relaxed; however, I have company fewer times.

Facing medical emergencies alone is downright scary. After my little heart event, which happened on April 1 (no fooling), every time I had a little pain like indigestion, a feeling of panic would rise up in my throat like reflux. I would keep my phone in my pocket, make sure the doors were unlocked or a key available in case ER workers needed to come in. One particular event left me shaking as I sat in my recliner and looked out over my beautiful back wooded area. God spoke to me through His word, "Fear not. Be not dismayed. I am your God. I will be with you and uphold you with my strong right arm" (Isa. 41:10). A peace came over me as I thought, *I don't need to fear. If my heart stops, I'm ready to go to Heaven. I'm not afraid to die.* From that time on, I've never once thought about being alone during an illness or if I had another heart event. Now, I have to talk to myself about taking precautions such as keeping phone numbers handy, meds close by, and doors locked. Praise God for good health to be able to work out at the gym faithfully and participate in several group activities such as cardio drumming. Praise God for His deliverance from fear.

The greeting card by Mary Engelbreit Ink says, "Worrying does not empty tomorrow of its troubles. It empties today of its strength."

We widows get stronger as the years go by. Granger Westberg sums our feelings of fear and growth in his book *Good Grief,* with these words.

> As we struggle to affirm reality, we find that we need not be afraid of the real world. We can live in it again. We can even love it again. For a time we thought there was nothing about life that we could affirm. Now the dark clouds are

beginning to break up, and rays of sun come through. And hope, based on faith in a God once more becomes a part of our own outlook on life.

This journey is filled with God's grace, comfort, and wisdom.

Suggestions for Going Places Alone

- Ask another single person to go with you to lunch or social gatherings.
- Ask for God's presence and comfort to go with you.
- Tell yourself that you might learn something or create new memories.
- Try going out to lunch where many people are alone such as a bakery or deli.
- Take your cell phone and catch up on email or messages.
- Visualize your loved one being with you…just don't talk aloud to him.
- Look around for someone else who is alone and say "Hello" or give a compliment.
- When at the gym, use your ear buds and cell phone to listen to uplifting music.
- Take three-by-five cards with Bible verse on them to the restaurant.
- Face time your grandchildren while you are eating lunch alone.
- When invited to a wedding, ask the person in charge if you can be seated with another single.
- Talk to some of your close couple friends about inviting two single people with another couple.

6

Waves of Depression

Even though my mother suffered from depression and my youngest son does, I really did not understand how debilitating it could be. Of course I had suffered some "down days," but nothing compared to this gut wrenching feeling of gloom and a feeling of being lost. I knew what I should do from reading books and counseling other people, but now that I was experiencing this deep wound, I learned how challenging those steps are. Little things could trigger a deluge of tears. One incident happened in April after Doug's passing in February.

My delightful and funny daughter-in-law invited me to go with her on a trip to a friend's home that was about four hours north where she would be singing and helping to make a recording. My heart sank as our hostess led me to my lovely room. I hope the expression on my face did not convey the desperation in my heart. This was the room where Doug and I had stayed the last time we visited. Struggling to gain control by breathing deeply and sending up one of those SOS prayers, I trudged up the stairs to hear my daughter-in-law calling her husband to tell him all about our trip—the frustrations of traffic, taking a wrong turn in Chicago, and desperately needing a bathroom. Rather than their laughter lifting my spirits, I realized that I had no one at home to call. If you are a widow reading this, you know this desolate feeling. Yet you want to be a part of others' joys so you do your best to "put on your happy face." That night as I tossed and turned, I cried out to the Lord having the assurance that He never gets tired of his children seeking Him. I didn't even know what to ask. I just knew I wanted that "terrible feeling" to go away. He came through. The next day at rehearsal, I was blessed and lifted as I heard the choir sing. One of my daughter-in-law's solos was "YOU ARE GOD" by Tammy Thurmond (our hostess). These words strengthened me.

> When the world around me crumbles and
> my fears are closing in, I have to CHOOSE
> To turn my eyes to you again. But even
> when my strength is weak, I need to lift my head,
> Lift my hands, lift my voice to you and say:
>
> Chorus: "You are God. You are my savior
> and my Lord. You are the Lamb who turns my
> fears to faith once more so I might live and
> walk on water to the One who always walks
> with me. You are God!
>
> Verse 2: On this journey I have traveled You
> have always led the way when I have trusted You
> In times I could not see. But Jesus, when my
> faith was weak, You said to lift my head,
> lift my hands, lift my voice to You and say

In the fall, I began to think of joining a grief share group. I told myself that I probably didn't need to go since I had read so many books on grief when I lost my dad, my mother-in-law, my two young brothers, and my mother. I really did not want to go and was afraid I would lose my composure or be bored. Pretty smug, huh? As I prayed about joining, that small still voice seemed to talk to me about my attitude and say, "Maybe you could be an encouragement to some-one else." I didn't even know how to find a group so Googled "Grief Share." Right in my community at a church down the road was a group called Grief Share International. I called the number of the facilitator who informed me she had only one person signed up so far. She wasn't sure how things would go. I asked her if we could pray together for others to sign up. This was in July and when I walked into the first meeting in September, I was not only greeted by this wonderful lady, I was blown away by God's answer to our prayer... fourteen people.

The only seat left was by a tall, quiet, and seemingly dignified young lady. We felt an instant connection as she told me that she hadn't wanted to come either. She had lost her sister and best friend a few months before. When she heard the radio announcement about Grief Share, she felt compelled (I believe that was the unction of the Holy Spirit) to sign up.

Beverly is an electrical engineer who had been transferred from Kentucky to Michigan. This was her first time to be away from her sister for years. She didn't even realize that her sister was that ill. Living alone in a new state had already sent Beverly into deep depression. Since she was such a quiet person, I was surprised that she opened up to me. I again had that gentle nudge from the Holy Spirit that this could be one of the reasons I was there. As we made more connections, she began to come to church with me. We have been friends now for eight years and even though she has moved back to Kentucky with her son and to care for her mom, we still talk every week. She is also a good listener and we often discuss strategies to overcome depression and work through our grief.

In her book, *Stunned by Grief,* Judy Brizendine tells of lady who felt she was drowning in grief so decided to go to a grief share group. After a few meetings, she expressed her feelings by saying, "I think it saved my life." Judy goes on to explain, "You may be tempted to close your heart to protect yourself, but the more you shut down to other people, the less alive you are." I can't recommend this Grief Share group enough. I even attended a second time three years later when the leaders at my own church asked me to lend a hand. I was amazed at how much more help I received as I was able to reflect on how far God had brought me on my journey. Some widows have expressed that they did not find help in a particular group. My suggestion would be to try another. Other widows have expressed that they need only God. Scripture tells us in Galatians 2:1 that we are to bear one another's burdens. Yes, we must seek God first; however, He created us for community. Yes, we take a risk; however, we eventually have someone with like experiences with whom to share. Our pangs of grief do not keep bouncing around within those walls of depression and can eventually find an escape.

My church family has been one of my greatest strengths. They have called me, helped me with household repairs, prayed with and for me, and invited me to dinner. Many of the books written about grieving widows indicate that depression sets in at the loss of couple friends. I have found this to be true in most cases but am thankful for those couples who have tried to include me. One of them asked me to go to dinner with them a few months after Doug's passing. Being a little hesitant to go, I talked to me self. (Yes, that's healthy.) "You should go. These are your dear, godly friends that you've had to your home many times, played games with, and prayed together. You would want one of them to come if the other had passed away." I also remember when Gayle lost her husband. I had practically begged her to join Doug and me and she refused until I finally asked, "Do you want to be my friend?" I didn't understand as I do now. We are still great friends today. So I did join my friends. Everything was good until I realized that we put all our coats and purses where Doug would have been sitting. Had to send up another SOS prayer. Then, there's always that time of saying good night and going home to an empty house. I've listed some ways to help with those feelings at the end of this chapter.

Amy describes her triggers of depression as hearing "their" favorite song or singing a favorite hymn at church. Since she and Brad often ate their dinner meals in a restaurant, she would see couples together and remember what fun she and Brad had experienced. Of course, she was happy for the couples, but experienced those sad feelings of "Where is my soul mate?" Teresa says going to dinners at church was difficult because everyone seemed to be with family and failed to invite her to sit with them. I, too, experienced a time when I looked around with my plate of food and just walked away and drove home. Now these are great people who love me, but I needed someone to invite me to sit with them. I was not angry because I realized that until I had experienced loss, I did not always do so well at including the single person. I knew they could not understand. Once we experience loss, we listen better; we spend more quality time with others. We pray more intently all the while hoping someone is praying for us or realizing that the only way we are making it through is because someone is praying. When our faith is faltering, the faith of others carries us. When we can't seem to pray, someone is praying for us.

Driving by their favorite coffee shop triggered Mary's feelings of sadness because she and Jack had spent many hours there in the neighborhood. Jack loved to tell people about his faith. He was like a magnet with his tall stature and unassuming nature. Right after the funeral, Mary began to think about one of the men Jack had been witnessing to at the coffee shop. Two days before Jack passed away, he had given one of his coffee buddies a copy of the devotional book, *Jesus Calling* by Sarah Young. Mary wondered what this pilot friend had thought about it, but she wasn't quite ready to go back to the coffee shop to find him so she began to pray for wisdom. While visiting the local hardware store that week, she looked up and there he was. With great excitement, he walked over to see her and wanted her to tell Jack how much he was enjoying the book. Of course, the tears erupted as she told him of Jack's passing. The pilot broke into tears as he expressed his deep gratitude for Jack and his friendship and his gratitude for the book, which he had been reading daily. As tears continued to roll down his cheeks, he explained that he had found new meaning for his life and had been taking the book with him as he flies around the country. Even in the depth of our sadness, God sends little rays of light.

Just realizing that these feelings are normal and will lesson with time gives hope, but it is hard to hold on to that hope. Gayle is a woman of deep faith and faithfulness to use her gifts for God, but when I talked with her two years after Lee died of a heart attack, she was so down that she told me she wished she could die. I remember feeling so alarmed that she had plunged into this deep depression, not even imagining how it would be until my own husband died. My husband and I kept asking. We even made a special trip while on vacation to visit her. Little by little, she would come to our home. Friends and family, please don't give up. Keep inviting, going by their home, sending cards, and of course, praying.

Another widow often said that she was sure the wrong parent had died because her adult children seemed so uncooperative and argumentative. Depression plagued her as they refused to visit her home where their dad had died saying they couldn't bear the sadness and that she could visit them if she was lonely. They only lived an hour away and she needed their help around the house. I tried to explain about their own grief and how challenging it is for adult children to grieve the death of a parent. Chapter 9 will give further insight concerning understanding the grief of the adult child.

One of the greatest helps for depression for me has been journaling. One of my friends gave me the devotional book, *Jesus Calling*, by Sarah Young on the day Doug passed. It has some blank spaces where I just jotted down my feelings. At one point, I told my pastor son that I felt my comments were too negative, and he assured me that was what made me seem so positive. I had already released those negative feelings. Writing them out surely helped me not to take them out on others. Joyce Brizendine writes, "Somehow you need to move your feelings from the inside to the outside so you can begin to face them, release them and start to heal." We don't always have someone with whom to talk or we are fearful that we will lose control. I kept journaling like this for eight years. I would compare what I had said the year before to see that sometimes I had made little progress, but overall, I was beginning to heal after about the third year. My entries became so much more positive and showed thankfulness for God's help. I began to realize how the power of the Holy Spirit was at work within me. "Out of His glorious riches He was strengthening me in my inner being" (Eph. 3:15b).

Several of the widows interviewed reported that one of the most difficult times was when they went home in the evening after visiting their adult children or just from a concert or a movie. The house seemed so empty and quiet. Attending weddings and the receptions afterward have brought pangs of sadness for several of the widows. Amy expressed that watching all the couples dance seemed to scream, "You are alone. You'll never have anyone with whom to dance again." Even going for a coffee can trigger sad feelings as most coupons are "buy one, get one free." There is no "free one." One of the young widows, Marcia explains how difficult it was to watch dads with their little ones and to see her friends having babies. Even through her sadness, she kept moving forward with her young son. They have been to Disney World twice and she has completed another college degree. In his book, *A Grace Disguised*, Jerry Sittser explains that it is not the experience of loss that becomes the defining moment of our lives. It is how we respond to loss that matters. After three years, while caring for her young son, Marcia is responding well.

As mentioned in chapter 4, widows of pastors remember hearing their husband's message each week and fellowshipping with parishioners both at church and in their homes. Not having that experience makes for an unbearable feeling of loneliness. I was blessed to have my pastor son and family close so did not experience those particular feelings; however, once they left, Sunday afternoon stretched before me. Doug and I had always taken a walk, talked about the great services, or just relaxed as we read books together. I tried some of the things on the list of "Depression Zappers" listed at the end of this chapter. I remember one Sunday afternoon going to the gym to work out and relax on the massage beds. That all-consuming blanket of grief began to weigh me down. When I confessed my negative feelings, I thought of a new young single girl who had recently moved to our city. She lived only ten minutes from the gym. At first, I thought, "She would not want to go with an older lady for pizza." Thankfully, the Holy Spirit's nudge continued. When I called, she was delighted. This pushing forward and stepping out of my comfort zone was probably more of a help to me than to her.

When do those waves of grief stop rolling over us and knocking us upside down? When will we stop crying? Jerry Sittser tells us that as the numbness of the death begins to wear off and life resumes, we need to make a choice to enter into a time of what some refer to as "a darkness." If we don't make a choice to enter into that darkness, we will never arrive at the light. Carol Brody, in her book, *Happily Even After*, states, "If you skip over any part of your life, at some time, you will go back to retrieve it." She goes on to say that many widows have unrealistic expectations. They are just certain they should not be crying after two or even three years. People tell us we are strong because *they* want us to be strong. We smile and think, "I surely don't feel strong. I knew I had to enter into that time of darkness. Oh, I didn't cry all the time in front of other people. I set aside a special time each evening as I sat by the fireplace. Sometimes, I cried so much, I felt empty. My head hurt. I actually told myself, "Stop! That's enough for tonight." I cried, prayed, read scriptures, felt devastated, at times hopeless...yet those tears eventually began to set me free. Memories went from hurting, to helping, to hoping to healing.

One of my couple friends told me about a rough time of grieving in their lives. A car accident had left their young daughter burned all over her body. She had to go through a process called "debridement" where her sores were actually opened to remove the dead tissue so healing could take place. Talk about pain proceeding healing! This didn't just happen once and done. It was a process just as mourning is. There are no specific steps. We don't move through denial once and for all. We don't get over anger once and for all. As C. S. Lewis expresses in his book, *A Grief Observed*, "For in grief nothing 'stays put.' One keeps on emerging from a phase, but it always recurs. Round and round. Everything repeats. Am I going in circles, or dare I hope I am on a spiral? But if a spiral, am I going up or down it." The open wound of grief allows God's healing. We definitely hurt before we heal.

The grief process is often taken with baby steps. It might be described as the following:

- A roller coaster with sharp twists and turns and sudden plunges. Your process can go from experiencing a smooth ride around a curve to a big jerk that makes you feel like your head is coming off.
- From enjoying calm waters to suddenly being turned upside down by a huge wave.

- Bumping up and down on a train as you enter a dark tunnel and coming out to the light again. You think there will be no more darkness, but then yet another tunnel.
- Enjoying the scenery on a nature trail when suddenly a wild animal jumps in front of you.
- A light pelting rain that turns into lightning and thunder.
- White water rafting that is going along okay and then a water fall or a tree stump emerges right in front of you.
- A journey into unknown territory without GPS. You ask, "Did I miss my turn? Am I going the right direction? Should I stop to ask for directions?"
- Being in an escape room…thinking you have found the way only to have a door slam in your face.
- Being wide awake in a pitch-black room or falling asleep in the middle of the day.

You can no doubt think of more. Grieving is our own journey. No one can do it for us. Other can help, but we have to keep moving forward. As I read a book *Getting to the Other Side of Grief* by Susan J. Zonnebelt-Smeenge and Robert C. DeVries, I thought, *I'm not sure there is another side. I will always grieve. I now know that I can walk through it with God's help, sometimes tiny steps, sometimes giant. The important thing is to keep going.*

Widows no not need to defend their sad feelings or explain why they can or cannot do things. Sometimes she just cannot face others. She may feel she is going crazy like Job might have felt in Job 3:26. "I have no peace, no quietness, no rest, but only turmoil." It's normal to do silly things like purchasing groceries and leaving them in the parking lot beside your car or driving somewhere and forgetting where you are going. Once, when I was finished at the gym, I climbed into the wrong car. It was the same model, but I thought I had locked my car, and I surely would not have left my wallet in the tray right in plain sight. I'm so thankful that God has a strong grip on us. "My soul clings to you. Your right hand upholds me" (Ps. 63:8).

Sometimes we fail to grieve because of other people's expectations. Some of the things people say make us wonder. Proverbs 25:20

gives insight. "Singing cheerful songs to a person with a heavy heart is like taking someone's coat in cold weather or pouring vinegar in a wound" (NLT). Some things might even be true, but are not appropriate such as the following:

- You are young so you will be able to marry again.
- You need to get out there again.
- Your deceased would not want you to be so sad.
- I know how you feel.
- Call me if you need anything.
- He's really better off and doesn't have to suffer anymore. (It might be okay for the widow to say this.)
- You won't need to take care of him anymore.
- "I'm sorry" might be overused.
- He's in a better place.
- How are you doing?
- At least he had a good and meaningful life.
- God must have needed him more that we do.

Better things to say might be the following:

- I feel so sad that your husband is not with us.
- I will really miss your husband.
- I remember when we…
- He was a remarkable person whom I won't forget. (Give an example.)
- He always made me laugh when we went fishing together.
- I love the way he laughed.
- I love the way he showed love to you by…
- He was a truly great friend to me as he…
- His influence will continue as we live and tell his story.

In the field of education, we learn that specifics are always better to say with children. Rather than saying "Good job" on an art project, we say, "I love the way you used different colors within each tree." The same is true with responses to grief. Of course, God gives us grace to see others' hearts.

When a widow cannot keep going or does not feel that strong grip, she must seek the help of a doctor, pastor, or therapist. Sometime medication is needed to work through the grief. Other times, we can just set goals or try new things. I've listed some things that we widows might try. Of course, we choose only one or two at a time. Cross the ones off that don't work and move on. The famous poet Emily Dickinson tells us, "Forever—is composed of Nows." Do something now even if it seems insignificant.

Depressions Zappers

1. Take a walk either outside or in the mall. Even though you might not talk to the people there, you are with others.
2. Try a gym membership. I love the one where I go that has massage beds. Ahh!
3. Get one of your teens, grandchildren, or a tech friend to show you how to make a playlist for your phone. You can play it while you walk or exercise.
4. Journal your feelings. If you don't like to write, draw pictures to depict your feelings.
5. Look through picture albums of happy times or of your babies or grandbabies.
6. Find a devotional book. Read one entry each day and tell how it makes you feel.
7. Write Bible verses/promises on three-by-five cards to read as you exercise or when you are in the car waiting on someone. Tape these around your house and read them every time you pass by.
8. Take a good book or your computer to a large book store in the evening.
9. Bake something for a neighbor or shut-in.
10. Read or listen to a good inspirational novel.
11. Sit in the library with others around reading magazines or working on your computer.
12. Sit by the fire and call a friend.
13. Watch a funny movie… Be careful not to watch some romantic movies that make you cry more.
14. FaceTime family members or friends.
15. Purchase a bouquet for your table.
16. Listen to a good Christian radio station on your way to work or in the morning when you are getting ready.
17. Write a letter/s to your loved ones capturing great memories or just look at his picture and tell him.

18. On special days such as your loved one's birthday or your anniversary, write a good memory or blessing for each year.
19. Use the alphabet to describe God or Jesus, such as A—almighty, aware of my needs, always present...
20. Try a new hobby such as playing a musical instrument or revisit an old hobby.
21. Volunteer at a food pantry or help with a children's educational class.
22. Join a group Bible study, craft, or activity group.
23. Get together with other widows and plan activities such as dinners in different restaurant or homes, movies, plays, or concerts.

7

More Traumatic Events

After going through a long illness and the care of one's husband or when death comes suddenly, a widow might think, *Surely, I can rest a little and take time to think things through.* Then bam! Another unimaginable catastrophe! Just a few months after Amy's husband passed from cancer, she was involved in a car accident that left her with a broken arm. Even though she had to return to work almost immediately, she had to deal with insurance claims and numerous doctor's visits. In addition to these events, Amy felt the stress of her daughter's divorce and eventual moving in with her until she could get on her feet financially. Amy's other daughter needed to move to another city further away, which left Amy feeling more alone and not being able to see her three young grandsons on a regular basis.

Right after Susie's husband, a retired elementary principal, died, she had to sell their gorgeous lake home, purchase another for the summer while maintaining her winter home in Arizona. Since this was before my husband passed, I helped her with the estate sale and move. Her grief was so fresh that she seemed to be moving in a trance. Another of her friends and I labeled things and tried to keep her on track with the packing…all the while listening to her expressions of bewilderment and sadness. We would even stop now and then to praise God for His strength and ask for His wisdom for the next step in Susie's life. The next year, she went through two major surgeries.

By this time, my husband had passed so I was able to fly to Arizona to help her for a week until her children could come. During all of this time, Susie was faithful to care for her ninety-seven-year-old mother. We kept sharing the promise found in Lamentations 3:22–23 (NIV): "Because of the Lord's great love, we are not consumed. His mercies are new every day. Great is His faithfulness."

Mary and her husband Jack always loved doing all their own yard work at their beautiful Cape Cod home. That first spring, Mary felt overwhelmed as she hauled away truckloads of leaves to prepare for spring planting. She tells a story of complete exhaustion as she had worked in the yard all day. She cried out to the Lord to strengthen her. About that time, she walked over to an area that she seldom saw and there, lying by the tree, was a bouquet of lilies, Jack's favorite. Comfort saturated her soul as tears of joy streamed down her face. None of her neighbors admitted to having placed them there. Early fall brought yet another challenge…two weeks of blizzard like conditions with a broken snow blower. Once again, God's provision came through as she prayed, "My God will supply all of my needs" (Phil. 4:19). Her son-in-law who lives one hour north was able to bring his truck and plow and several neighbors pitched in to help.

After the sudden death of Lee, Gayle was left with no life insurance, no close family in the area, and a huge house payment. This forced her to put her house up for sale and make all the decisions that go along with that. Eventually, she had to sell at a loss. Can you believe that at her estate sale, some people were trying to "fix her up" with a widower. I'm sure they meant well, but that was the last thing on her mind after having just lost her soul mate a few months before. Being completely uprooted and having to live in another state with her son caused considerable anxiety and having to completely rely on God's strength and provision. She was able to get a job as a retail manager with many hours, but she stuck with it. It's no wonder she called and told me she didn't want to go on with her life anymore. God did provide and she was able to lease a house soon. During this time, her other son left his wife and family and stopped communicating with her. Twelve years later, she gives a strong testimony. She describes her feelings of depression as a battle that required having to face each day with a determination to fight. She tells how a turning point came when she expressed to her adult son that she wanted to take her own life. Feeling at the end of his rope in dealing with her, he asked, "Why don't you just do it, Mom? It surely couldn't hurt us more than what you are doing now."

When Kim's husband died, her college-age daughter began to have panic attacks and her older newly married daughter moved to Germany. She tells of being in such a state of shock as her young husband died suddenly of a heart attack. Driving three hours to where her daughter was in college was all a blur. When she and her sister-in-law told the daughter of her father's death, she screamed and left the dorm room running all over the campus. Rather than Kim's being able to come to grips with her own grief, she needed to console and help her daughter. She has always been a woman who put others first; however, in the next few years, she had to deal with her grief as she sold a house, bought a condo, and changed jobs. She reports victory through daily surrender. Even though she often felt tired and weary, she knew from Isaiah 40:28b, "He (God) will not grow tired or weary and his understanding no one can fathom. He gives strength to the weary and increases the power of the weak" (NIV).

Lori had known for about a year that Rod might die from cancer. She had spent every day and most nights with him in the hospital at various times for two years. Her anticipatory grief seemed to be helping her until his relatives came to the house and asked her to move out. The home had originally been in their mother's name; however, Lori had documents to prove the home had been placed in Rod's name years before and Rod had made many improvements over the years even though they had been living in a different state. One of Rod's sisters even took most of Lori's jewelry that was worth thousands. Lori had to involve the police and press charges while she was still in shock from Rod's passing. She did eventually recover most of the jewelry and other items that had been taken. Her own son took all of his father's guns which were quite valuable. When confronted, he told his mom that his name was the same as his dad's and that was all he had left of him. She had to decide which was more important, the guns or her relationship with her son. She chose to forgive and allow him to have the guns knowing that God would provide for her in other ways.

As mentioned in chapter 4, I began to experience extreme fatigue and what I thought was my regular reflux disease experienced since childhood. Just a few months after Doug passed, I was trying to paint one of my small bathrooms and would have to keep getting down off the ladder to rest. Hardly able to hold my arms above my head to paint the ceiling, I would get down and think, "Wow! I didn't realize how challenging it must have been for Doug to do so many paint jobs around our home over the years." He had even painted the whole kitchen the last week before he went into the hospital. A few months before, I'd had a stress test that showed some discrepancies, but I just laughed it off since I had no history of heart disease in my family, I was not overweight and exercised daily. I really wasn't concerned that my cholesterol was 279 because my grandmother's always ran high and she lived to be 88. The cardiologist who read my results even said I probably did not need to rush into anything, but I might want to have a CAT scan. I even put that off until after Doug died. Oh, the crazy things we do when we are grieving! The results showed that I probably needed an angioplasty. When I finally had it done in a few months, the results showed a 90 percent blockage in my left descending artery, which called for two stents. The doctor reported that my heart was in great shape, but a clot from the blockage could have cause a major problem. God shows grace even when we don't realize we need it. Psalm 46:1 (NIV) assures us, "God is our refuge and strength, an ever present help in trouble."

My recovery went well, and I even moved furniture two days after (with slider furniture movers). My kids were aghast as I told them the doctor told me to do whatever I felt like…just not to lift over 20 pounds for a few days. I didn't. I just slid the furniture. Well, maybe it was over twenty pounds when I used the tool to lift the book case up to put the sliders in place. My son only lives five minutes down the road, but my stubborn independence sometimes gets in the way. I did begin to develop some anxiety every time I had a little indigestion pain thinking, "Well, I didn't know I had blockage before. Maybe something else is wrong. I remember sitting in my chair by the fire during my regular "set aside" grieving time and thinking, *I cannot live in fear. I'm going to trust you, God, to be my companion and give me peace.* Zephaniah 3:17 gave me courage. "The Lord your God is with you. He is mighty to save. He will take great delight in you. He will quiet you with His love" (NIV). He did and I can honestly say that I have no anxiety concerning my heart. I went through cardiac rehab with flying colors and one of the nurses there told me that she thought my blockage might have been caused by stress, and I would probably have no more trouble. I did lose ten pounds and lowered my salt intake which has kept me from taking any medications except the lowest dose of a Statin drug for eight years now. I'm happy my last cholesterol reading was 179.

Something worse than a heart event happened in the next few months. My middle son and his family decided to attend another church. Now you might be saying, "Well, you should be happy they even wanted to go to church." I was, but I had just lost their dad and now I felt I was losing them. I felt betrayed that my son would leave the denomination that his dad and I had given our lives to and where his brother was the pastor. I could no longer look forward to having my little guys run to greet me and sit with me every Sunday morning. I cried many tears as I asked God to give me patience and understanding. They continually raved about their brother's preaching but said they needed more autonomy…a new start since they had not been married very long. This son had lost his first wife to cancer and his new wife had adopted his two young sons. You are probably already seeing some reasons they might have made the decision to change churches. I wasn't feeling it, but God gave me the strength to continue having them over for dinner once per week, grading my daughter-in-law's papers (she taught the same grade/subject that I had taught) and later to care for their new baby one day per week. I was the one who needed to change, wait, and pray. I had to commit them to God and His grace as the Apostle Paul states in Acts 20:32. "Now I commit you to God and to the word of His grace which can build you up" (NIV).

One year later, when they moved to a new city for professional reasons, they needed a place for my two older grandsons who needed to finish their last six weeks of school. My son would come on some weekends for their sporting events. On one occasion, we began to talk about their new church in their new city. I expressed my joy at their spiritual growth. My son began to talk about their moving to a different church after their dad died. The door opened for my expressing sadness about the issue. Tears began to roll down my son's face as he said, "Mom, why didn't you say something? I would not have left." I told him how thankful I was that I had listened to the Holy Spirit to keep silent because God had truly been working in their lives. Perhaps if he had kept coming to church with me, they would not have grown the way they had. I would not have grown. Once again, I was reminded that God's plan might be different from mine. "For my thoughts are not your thoughts, neither are your ways my ways declares the Lord. As the heavens are higher than the earth, so are my ways higher than your ways" (Isa. 55:8, 9 NIV).

Surely, things would stay calm for this grieving widow! Of course not! While visiting with this family in their new city four hours away, I began to hear a noise in the back wheel of my little Ford Escape. Even my grandsons mentioned the noise as I drove all over that large metropolitan area to take them golfing and to game and eating places. We thought the noise might be bottles rolling around in the back area. The next day, as I drove over 70 mph on Hwy 94 for my return trip, the noise grew louder. Feeling close to a panic attack, I cried out to the Lord for wisdom. My car seemed to just automatically turn into a rest stop where I saw only one person, a burly-looking truck driver. My prayers turned to, "Oh, Lord, I pray he is an angel in disguise." Even though he did not look like one, I pulled over to where he was standing and asked if he would look at my tires. Can you just imagine being alone in a rest top with a strange man? He stooped down, and after a few minutes, his face appeared in my window as he uttered some choice words. I tried to be brave as he told me it was a wonder I was alive. "You have only two lug nuts in your tire and the other ones are loose. What kind of idiot worked on your car?" He stayed with me until Triple AAA came to haul me to the nearest repair place. Thankfully, my car was repaired within two hours at no charge. Thank God for cell phones, angels in disguise, and His marvelous grace.

Since I had never taken care of a home alone, I was clueless what to do when my lovely little condo was invaded by chipmunks who had gotten in under the foundation. To my dismay, my HOA moved extremely slowly so I purchased large traps and caught seven before the problem was finally solved. I couldn't bear seeing those cute little furry creatures in the trap so my son offered to come over each night to put them to rest in the woods behind my condo. One of the men from my church came over to make sure there were no openings around the foundation of the then unfinished basement. While he was working, he left an opening for a few minutes while he went to his truck to retrieve a tool. When he came back, he found that a little red squirrel had gotten in. What a sight to see Jim chasing the squirrel with a curtain rod and eventually pushing him from behind the TV to the escape hole.

Even this last spring when I had to fly home from Arizona early due to the COVID pandemic, I was greeted with little field mice. I had never set a mouse trap, much less emptied one. The whole time, I am saying, "You can do this, Paula. They are just little critters." The night before, a baby mouse ran across the throw I had covered my feet with. Another ran up the drape and perched at the top of my curtain rod as if he were staring at me. I set a trap at the bottom and within an hour, he ran right down for the cheese as I watched. Someone said he must have been sitting up there contemplating suicide. Others asked, "How could you sleep that night?" I didn't, but by the next day, my HOA manager came over and discovered the hole around the foundation where they had entered. Haven't seen another for years.

One of the most difficult things I had to deal with was helping my youngest son with his addictions. He had been sober for eight years before his dad died; however, around the same time as his dad's death, he was experiencing relational and employment problems. He stayed with me for a few weeks, but it became evident to me that he needed to leave. The breaking point was one evening when I was sitting quietly waiting for him to come home. The Holy Spirit brought to my mind some pain pills that had been prescribed for me when I had a minor surgery. I had only taken one and put the others up in the cabinet to dispose of in the proper places. The week before, I had been looking for cold and sinus medicine while my son was in the room and no doubt saw the pills. I knew immediately to look, and yes, they were gone. I began to pray again, and God brought to my mind where my son might be. He had earned many points for five-star hotels through his job. Even though I had called his cell phone several times with no answer, I called one more time and this time left this message, "Son, I know where you are, and if you do not answer this call, I will call the police to come with me to get you because you should not be driving." He did pick up and insisted on driving home. He later asked me how I knew where he was. One might ask, "If God can tell you where he is, why doesn't he prevent this 'out of control' life?" I really don't know the answer to that. I do believe God heals and restores, but I also know, His timing is not mine. "I say to myself, 'The Lord is my portion: therefore, I will wait for him'" (Lam. 3:24 NIV).

When my son arrived, he became irritable and unkind, which was truly out of character for him. When I had to be really firm with him, he became rude and said he would be leaving with his two dogs. I told him that I thought that was not a good idea, but if he did, to please leave the house key and the garage door opener on the counter, and that if he did not, I would change the locks on the doors. I went back to my room, sat in my prayer chair, and wept and prayed until the wee hours. After some sleep, I awoke to his being on the phone with a local rehab center to reserve a bed. There's the miracle—a new beginning. I do wonder how I helped to make all these arrangements on a holiday weekend. A fellow widow friend went with me to take him to the center, which was one hour north. I cry even now as I think about seeing my gorgeous six-foot son bend over in shame as I left him there in that place. Since this was mostly a temporary place, he flew to another facility for long time care. After a year of rehab and living in a sober house, he felt ready to take a job in Florida.

During the rehab time, I kept his two dogs. I am not a dog person, but loving my son immensely, I did my best to be patient. One dog was a beautiful fourteen-year-old silky and the other an eight-month old puppy mix of Russel Terrier. Taking them out for daily procedures was a challenge due to the hyper puppy and impatient older dog. Keep in mind, this was in the middle of Michigan winter weather. I'm so thankful for God's help with even the little things. Friends came through to help me with training the puppy to be more gentle and not bark so much and one friend and her husband even puppy sat for me when I went to visits to my son or meetings for parents of those suffering with addition. One bitterly cold evening, I was cooking for a family who had lost a relative. The phone rang, and with my level of stress concerning my son as well as not being accustomed to caring for two dogs, I was caught up in my phone conversation and forgot about heating the grease to cook the steak in. I looked up to see smoke from the kitchen, rushed in, removed the pan from the stove, threw flour on the flames, and opened the back door. Out zoomed the little hyper puppy. After calling and calling, I went back in the house to make sure the other dog was okay, bundled up for the below-freezing weather and called my dog lover friend, Pat. Can you imagine, these two little old ladies all bundled up walking up and down the icy street called, "Maybeline." Yes, that was her name.

Feeling totally frustrated and freezing, I muttered complaints as I looked under the bushes in front of my condo. That still small voice whispered, "I'm here. Just ask." I repented of my attitude and asked God to give me direction. Immediately, the thought came into my mind, "Take the other dog with you to look for her." Just across the street, a little frozen whimpering puppy emerged and went right to my dog-loving friend, Pat. One might be thinking, *What a crazy thing to do? Leave a pan of hot grease on the stove.* I know I'm being vulnerable here, but I have a sneaky suspicion, many widows under stress have done similar things. If not, a time will come, and she will know that she is not alone and that God cares about all of our circumstances. I praised the Lord as I cleaned the black off my stove. (There is still a spot there to remind me of God's protection.) Not only did God answer my prayer for forgiveness, he reminded me of his faithfulness to protect me. Sitting right beside the hot burner was the bottle of cooking oil that was beginning to melt. Not only have I been much more careful, I've had new smoke detectors installed and purchased fire extinguishers.

During all this time, I was invited to attend meetings for family members of those suffering with addition. This meant an hour drive in Michigan winter weather to the rehab facility. What an experience! At every meeting, I engaged with twenty or more parents, many of whom had lost all hope for their loved ones. Again, I asked, "God, how can I do this without Doug? How can I learn and how can I encourage others as you have encouraged me?" Boy, did he ever show me? First, I did learn so much. I read at least fifteen books with one of them presenting the exact picture of my mother whom I wrote about in chapter 1. As I read, I realized what a miracle her healing was in the year before she passed at age sixty-six. Each meeting began with, "Hello, I am [insert name], and I have a son who is an addict." Your typical AA meeting style. After having made connections with many of the people, I heard little hope. Even though credit was given to a "Higher Being," I felt such sadness that so few gave testimony of any hope. Even though I was a little hesitant to mention Jesus, I took a big breath and said, "My name is Paula. I have a son who is an addict, and I had a mother who was an addict but was delivered and healed: therefore, I have hope in my God for my son's future." The room became very quiet and the facilitator who, of course, had to be politically correct, expressed thanks for my sharing and went on with the meeting. After the meeting, I was practically thronged by several people who hugged me and thanked me for sharing. One couple said they had wanted to share their faith, but were hesitant. To God be the glory!

Just when life seems to be going better, we face another curve. As I walked out of the building that night, I was greeted with heavy winds and snow. I did have an umbrella, but my boots were in the car, which was parked in the back of the building where the darkness had engulfed the landscape. As I finally located my car and climbed in with soggy feet, I began to wonder if I should try to get a hotel, but then I remembered the dogs. I had to give it a try so I called my pastor son and told him my plans. He promised to pray and call every twenty minutes to make sure I was okay. Having lived in Pennsylvania and New York, I knew how to drive in the snow, but this appeared to be more dangerous. Fighting the wind to keep in my lane, I prayed fervently for God to be my navigator. The semitruck in front of me was my only indication of where the white line of my lane might be. I kept calling out to the Lord like in Psalm 50:15. "Call upon me in the day of trouble. I will deliver you and you will honor me." With his help and protection, I made the forty-five-minute trip in two hours. Thankfully, that was my last meeting, and I was able to glean so much information to help myself and others over these past few years.

Once again in our humanness, we think, "Things are going smoothly." Another wave comes, but we are stronger. God is helping us to keep those spiritual muscles developed. My son was sober and clean from drugs for over two years. He felt he was able to take another job as a CPA in another state. Being a great distance from family, he relapsed once again. This time, he came to a crisis experience in his faith as he was staying at my home. He went back into rehab for two years and secured a job. Before he totally relapsed, he called for financial help, which I knew I could not give mostly because it would enable him. My older son and I flew to where he lived, closed up the rental house, found a home for the dogs, and brought him to my home. In a loving and compassionate way, we assured him that this would be the last time we rescued him.

The scripture, "Fear not, be not dismayed, I am your God. I will uphold you with my strong right arm" (Isa. 41:10, NIV) kept going through my mind as I was terrified of flying alone from Michigan to Florida to help my son. My oldest son insisted on getting his own flight and meeting me there. This calmed me somewhat as I packed one personal item and one carry on. My carry on had to be left at the curb due to a full flight. I thought, "Good, I don't have to be concerned about lifting it to the overhead compartment. Thank you, God." A young lady right in front of me was struggling so I asked a young man to help her. Not knowing she was the person God had placed in my life to encourage that day. (That's one of my daily prayers: "Lord, send someone across my path to encourage or be encouraged by.) With tears in her eyes, she expressed her gratefulness. When we arrived, I had to wait in the little hall area for my bag. She came over to me and told me again how thankful she was because her husband had passed only a few months later and this was so scary to fly alone. While talking to her, I grabbed my little blue bag without checking the tag.

As we walked through the large airport on the way to the second leg of the flight, she gave me her card as a local realtor. I assured her that I would be praying and perhaps we would meet again in our hometown. While walking, I heard someone yelling, "Hey, you with the blue bag. That's my bag." I looked down, and sure enough, the tag did not have my name on it. Surely no one else had a small royal blue bag just like mine. She practically ripped the bag from my hand as I asked where my bag was. "Oh, I left it back at the gate." I ran all the way back only to be told that the bag had already been put back on the plane and that I should go to the help desk when I arrived in Miami and they would help me track it down. Just what I needed! Again, I quoted, "Fear not, I am with you."

I texted my son who was meeting me in Miami, that I would be at the desk downstairs. The attendant was very helpful when I described the suitcase and its contents and told me it would be in the next day. That definitely would not help since we were leaving to drive back to Michigan, and it was a two-hour drive through traffic back to the airport. I had them locate the suitcase and fly it back to Kalamazoo. That meant I had to wear the same clothes for three days and was missing some items to make me more comfortable at my youngest son's home and the two stops on the way home. God doesn't always answer our prayers in exactly the way we think, but he does stay with us and help us. I was so thankful that I had the most essential items in the small bag I had taken as my personal item. The bag did arrive in Kalamazoo in five days with only one broken item... my beloved travel hairdryer...so minor in the scheme of things!

When we finally arrived at my youngest son's home in Miami, the two little dogs were yapping as they searched for their master. Pushing the unlocked door open revealed their lack of care but their joy to reunite with me. My son had left his truck there when he took a taxi to the nearby hospital to regain some sense of sobriety. Only one problem: no keys and how would we get him and begin to pack up? We searched everywhere, asking God to show us where they might be. Words came into my mind, "Look upstairs in the pockets of his jeans." Sure enough, a pair of jeans was under the bed with the keys in the pocket. Another miracle that he had not taken them with him! My older son went to get his brother while I stayed there in this huge house alone with the dogs. We did have our cell phones, but those anxious thoughts began to creep in. "What if he gets lost? What if he has an accident? What would I do?" Fear not... Fear not... Fear not..." continued to resonate in my mind.

God was truly with us as we drove my son's Chevy Tahoe filled to the brim, all the way back to Michigan. Knowing he might have severe withdrawal from alcohol, drugs, and nicotine. I prayed continually in the back seat as my pastor/counselor son talked and listened to his brother. What a miracle as the only sign of any withdrawal was a restlessness. We even stopped at a friend's house to spend the night. No shakes. No convulsions. No panic attacks. That's a miracle.

After arriving at my home, he would sit on the couch and read his AA Big Book. He also attended meetings continually but still took no depression meds or consumed alcohol. During this time, he was waiting on his severance pay from the previous job and making arrangements for rehab. He explains a real turning point or crisis experience as he was sitting on the couch in my living room one afternoon. I was in my bedroom on my knees, praying for another miracle.

Complete healing did not come in an instant, but I knew God was working when my son told me that while he was reading his AA book, a feeling of peace came over him as he had a deep impression of these words in his mind. "Andrew, you've never given over your life completely to anyone or anything except yourself." He went on to say that he began to wrestle with what that meant on a day-to-day basis. He knew he must surrender both right then and daily. His severance check came the next day, and he had arrangements made to go back into long-term rehab. After a year of being drug- and alcohol-free while working at a minimum-wage job, he secured a job in his professional field as a CPA. He did so well that he was offered an even better job. We are thinking, "This is it. He will not struggle again." Again, God did not answer in the way we thought. Unusual circumstances ended the new job—layoffs with the economy and COVID-19 pandemic. Yes, we could be discouraged, but we praise God that he has not turned to drugs or alcohol. Will he get another job? Will he struggle with depression? Maybe, but he is pressing on. Psalm 42:16b gives us hope for anything that might come along. "I will turn the darkness into light and make the rough place smooth" (NIV).

First Peter 4:12 tells us in the Living Translation to *not* be surprised at the fiery trials that we are going through, but we *are* surprised. "How can anything else bad come along?" It's kind of like when someone says, "Cheer up. Things could get worse." So you cheer up, and they do get worse. James 1:2 even says, "Consider it pure joy when you face trials." How does a widow do that when she faces fears like the following:

- Dying alone
- Making a poor financial decision
- Not having enough money
- Children and grandchildren not wanting to come visit or making poor decisions
- Going places alone
- Spending holidays alone
- Getting ill in the middle of the night
- Forgetting things like an appointment or paying a bill
- Emergency home repairs like the air conditioning going out

In her study on Elijah and spiritual stamina, Melissa Spoeltra calls this "what if" list "toilet bowl thinking," which, of courses, needs to be flushed. Our natural tendency is to fear. Sheila Walsh in her book, *It's Okay Not to Be Okay* has a great acronym for us. Fear is

- false
- evidence
- appearing
- real

God's word is the opposite. He tells us to put our trust in him no matter the circumstance. We keep moving forward and "Do the next thing." When another big wave comes along, we take a big breath and remember how God has been there for us. We have hope. Barbara Johnson, in her book *Pack Up Your Gloomies in a Great Big Box.* gives her definition of hope. "Hope is the feeling you get when you know the feeling you have won't be forever." Our hope is in God, our maker, our husband, friend, confidant, sustainer, comforter, creator, rock, fortress, guide, and the horn of our salvation. Psalm 55:22 instructs us. "Cast your cares upon the Lord and He will sustain you, He will never let the righteous fall" (NIV). That just means when we feel like we are falling, we cry out to Him. Then we visualize his strong right arm grasping us and holding on to us until our feet reach solid ground again.

Suggestions for Coping When More Struggles Come

1. Don't panic.
2. Go for a walk and think about God's goodness in other areas of your life.
3. Refer to your journal to see how God has brought you through other rough times.
4. Find a support group.
5. Continue your depression zappers.
6. See a good counselor/therapist.
7. Don't talk to everyone about how rough your life is—just a trusted friend or group.
8. Reach out to someone else who might be going through a tough time.
9. Find promises in the Bible about God's strength and wisdom.
10. When facing a decision, make a list of pros and cons or possible solutions.

8

Ministering to Others

Those who have recently become widowed might read this title and think, "What? Minister to others? I need someone to minister to me." Some may say, "Bring it on. Then I don't have to think about being so lonely." These thoughts represent two groups…those who are either overly committed or those who are too overwhelmed to think about reaching out to others. Either of these categories is acceptable. We need time to evaluate our particular personalities, our desires, energy levels, the needs of others, and to listen for God's instructions. Widows sometimes express their lack of faith and inability to even pray. Second Timothy 2:13–15 comforts us, "Even when we are too weak to have any faith left, He (God) remains faithful to us and will help us, for he cannot disown us who are part of himself, and he will always carry out his promises" (NIV). Hopefully, readers will make connections with these stories of other widows and be able to either start or continue their journeys.

Doug and I were always a ministry team. Even though I taught school full time, I was greatly involved in teaching classes at church for children and adults. In addition, we welcomed guests into our home on a regular basis. We would plan the menus together and he would help as much as his schedule allowed. When people came, he always involved our sons in the serving and clean up. Many times, we had people for games and snacks. Without him, who would want to come? I had to shift my focus to single women. I figured out how to have couples together by having another widow friend come early to help. I also enjoy having my pastor son and his family with new families from the church. I find that I cannot entertain as often as I used to, but I can at least aim for once per month. I pray for wisdom to know how much and when. I simply could not just quit using my gift of hospitality. In the beginning of my grief journey, I often whined about not being included in the group/couple fellowships at church because as a married person, I had always tried to invite single people. I finally decided I could complain. "Do all things without murmuring and complaining" (Phil. 2:14 NIV) or I could ask God to help me with a better plan. I was really spoiled because Doug always made a big deal of everything I did. Could I live without all those accolades? Learned something else about myself. God is enough.

One of the first children's ministry opportunities for me was our district family camp. I was asked to train ten college helpers, develop learning stations, and teach all the Bible lessons to over one hundred children. Normally, I was able to bounce off all my ideas on Doug and he would help me haul things and set up elaborate scenery and objects for the stories. Sometimes, he would even be a part of a skit or story. As the time grew closer for family camp to happen, I began to panic. How would I do it? Only in the strength of the Lord. It was really difficult, but I was committed or did I need to be "committed"? Perhaps I should have prayed more for wisdom before making my decision. I was told my work was for only this summer because I would be training the younger women to take over. Sounded good until I was overwhelmed with securing curriculum and materials.

I look back and think, "You were crazy to take that on." Maybe I was, but even in our stupidity or over eagerness to help, God comes through. Services were held every morning and evening with over one hundred children participating. I had a wonderful assistant, another retired teacher, to help set up the learning stations. The children learned memory verses as they played games and participated in activities in the stations. One of the young children's pastors on the district did all the music as I worked on keeping order and participation. Even though God really helped me, I was exhausted the next week. We do learn from these experiences. He does work for the good in all situations (Rom. 8:26). The kids and the college students learned, the young adults were ready to take on the ministry the next summer, and I knew God had truly given me strength.

In the few months before Doug passed, we had begun co-teaching a group of around fifty adults on Sunday evenings. It was supposed to be a twelve-week study on the Holy Spirit. Around the middle of the study, Doug became too ill to teach, so I took over. I probably should have had someone else take over, but again, I was committed or maybe a little crazy…again! Attendance fell off a little, which discouraged me, but I knew some were really experiencing growth. In January, the weather did not permit our meeting for several times and attendance fell off more. Even after Doug's passing in February and the attendance plunging down to around fifteen, I kept going. Once again, my stubbornness and pride won out. God not only helped me to grow spiritually, he showed me to wait more on him and seek his wisdom in further decisions about ministry. I continually pray as the psalmist David, "Show me your ways, Lord, teach me your path. Guide me in your truth and teach me for you are God my savior and my hope is in you all day" (Ps. 25:4–5).

While still in a state of shock over the loss of Doug, I learned that one of the families where we had last ministered lost their eighteen-year-old son. Spencer has just rededicated his life to God and was turning in a whole new direction away from drugs. His parents, faithful and loving members of the church, were so excited to see this radical change. Only one month later, Spencer was on his way home from a school event when he lost control of his truck and was killed instantly when he hit a mammoth tree. I knew I had to go, but should I? In somewhat of a trance, I got in my car to go to the Christian bookstore to purchase a card and a gift. On the way there, my ears picked up the sound of a siren. "Oh, dear, someone must be speeding." Guess what? I was the one the officer pulled over.

In a professional and kind voice, he asked if I knew how fast I was going. I assured him that I did not know, and when he saw the tears in my eyes, he thought I was upset about his pulling me over.

I explained where I was going and why, to which he was graciously attentive. He asked, "How is your driving record?" I responded that I had never had a ticket, but I probably deserved one. He went back to his patrol car and returned with his infamous tablet. To my utter amazement, he only issued a warning and told me to be careful on my way to minister to the family who had lost their son. Taking a deep breath, I began to praise God for his protection and asked him to help me think more clearly as I searched the right words or ways to comfort this family.

After overextending myself several times, I finally learned to seek God's will more fervently and to realize I don't have to do all the ministries I formerly did. God is helping me to find new ministries. Sometime I have to say "no" in order to say "yes" to a different path. After two years of just concentrating on my health and my family, I began to have a burden for the ladies in our church. After arriving home from a restful and exhilarating beach vacation with another widow and two couple friends, I approached a precious retired pastor's wife in our church. At almost the same time, we said, "I want to talk to you about a ladies' prayer and share group." Now, that was waiting on the Lord and understanding His will for ministry. We began that fall with about six ladies, and now three years later, we have met for two twelve-week sessions per year with an average attendance of twenty. Unfortunately, the retired pastor's wife is no longer able to help, but many ladies have stepped up to the plate to facilitate small groups within the group. Other ministries such as food pantry, outreach to abused women, help in nursing homes, and mission work have emerged. The ladies faithfully pray and encourage each other while they participate in other ministries of the church and community.

I am blessed to attend so many community events where I have opportunity to share Doug's testimony. People will always open the conversation with a way that he blessed them, and I am able to share God's wonderful provision for me and the story I shared in chapter 2 of his conversion. Just recently, I had a repairman in my home who asked about Doug's profession. That led to my telling him the story and the repairman shedding tears and thanking me for increasing his faith. One of the professors where I taught as an adjunct, wanted to know about Doug's life. Even though she is a Christian, she, too, expressed the help she received from his testimony. Of course, I have many opportunities to share with my three adult sons and my five grandsons. They loved Papa, and it is now my ministry to continue the legacy of his faith. I'm glad I'm there to tell them what I feel Papa would have said. Sometimes I wonder why Doug had to die first, and then I remember that he was a man of few words. God wants me to continue telling the stories.

God often uses us in the most unusual times and circumstances. While in the emergency room for a minor mishap, the doctors insisted that I forego a test on my heart just to make sure everything was working properly. One of the nurses looked so familiar to me and seemed to want to talk. When I asked how long she had worked for this particular hospital, she responded that she had only been in this department for two years; however, she had previously been on the cancer floor for seventeen years. As we talked, she remembered our family and being Doug's nurse on his last stay before he died. I told her that my son, who was with me, and I were people of faith and that we pray often. Then I asked, "When we pray, is there anything we could remember for you?" With tears in her eyes, she responded, "Yes, please pray for my family and that God will help me continue to be effective on my job."

Mentoring other widows and other single women has been one of my main ministries. At first, I just wanted someone to encourage me. Then I found that as I reached out to others, I was greatly encouraged. That still small whisper seem to say, "You know how it feels when people don't reach out to you. Make a difference in someone else's life." Even though I was a pastor's wife and extrovert, I still struggled to reach out because when I had tried before with Gayle, she seemed to push me away. That was before I had suffered a similar grief. I could not really identify. Now, it's almost instant connection. I say almost because some are still hesitant to talk with anyone or be with anyone. I have never been a phone talker... I like face to face, but that is often difficult. I recently had two college friends widowed who both live in different states. I had not spoken with Jennifer since college, but when I saw her post on Facebook, I knew I needed to try. She had lost Joe just a few months before. Yes, she cried. I cried, but through it all, she was so thankful for my calls. Another former missionary friend, and I discovered how many things we have in common. She is writing a book about her missionary journeys after the loss of her sweet Robert.

Although I still don't like to talk on the phone, I spend about five hours per week doing just that. FaceTime and speaker phone are such a help. When one of my widow friends was here visiting for a week just one year after her husband passed, my son was also here. He exclaimed, "Mom, you surely are patient." When I asked why, he replied, "You listen to your friend telling the same story over and over." I gently explained to him that widows or anyone going through grief need someone to tell the same story...sometimes just to diffuse and sometimes to convince themselves that this is really happening." In her book, *When People Grieve*, Paula D'Arcy explains, "Telling the story is a mental trying-on. It's a process of taking an enormous reality and breaking it up into pieces small enough to fit inside of you. It's a way of taming something wild and unruly until it becomes manageable."

Another ministry in which God helped me to see that I needed to go another direction was children's quizzing. I was the storyteller for a group of twenty-five children, ages five to eleven, on Wednesday evenings. Oh sure, I can tell a great story, but keeping all ages interested and engaged proved to be more of a challenge than I could handle along with my grief, working part-time, and handling all the home responsibilities. First of all, the children were tired after having been in school all day, compounded by my own fatigue. They loved the stories and begged me to stay, but I knew my patience was wearing thin when I was irritable with one of the older boys one evening. I apologized to him and his mom who graciously accepted and forgave. While I knew God would make His strength show up in my weakness, I also knew that He was pointing me in another direction. Others who had watched me tell the stories and help the children learn stepped up to the plate and I began to concentrate more on other ministries. Am I glad I put in all the hours for backdrops, memory games, and writing skits? Yes, because others were being trained and now not a Sunday goes by that I don't hear a little voice calling, "Ms. Paula, I learned my memory verse." It's almost like getting a hug from my Heavenly Father.

With my work in children's ministry, I was really limited in my ability to participate in music activities in the church. Now, I am free to play in the church orchestra on a regular basis. I also have more time to participate in the early morning prayer meetings and greeting people on Sunday mornings. One of the best books I have read on grief is by Gerald L. Sittsers entitled *A Grace Disguised*. His words confirm, "Our grief can send us in different directions as we trust and wait on the Lord. Sure, we hurt, cry and wonder, 'What is my new normal?' But we keep waiting, listening, and taking one step forward. We can become so much stronger than we ever imagined."

Amy was in full time ministry when Brad died. Even though her church was generous and loving, she needed to get up every Sunday to lead worship. Only God's grace and strength could help her continue to lead in worship and be the church administrator. A few years later, she did realize that she had put her grief on hold and had to really work through more struggles. We do what we have to do if we are a working widow. After three years, she was able to sell her home and move to a place where she can rest a little. She still works part-time but is not in charge of so many things. With her loving nature and organizational skills, she is already finding new ministries of getting other single ladies together for social events. This past Valentine's Day, we "Galentines" enjoyed an amazing and beautiful meal and game time. On Saturdays, she organizes musical times with groups of people who live nearby. Amy also ministers to her children and their families. She often has one of her five grandchildren spend the weekend.

While Amy was in the process of moving three years after Brad has passed, she stayed with me for a week as I recuperated from major surgery. Wow! God leads us in all kinds of exciting ways. One night when I called to check on her (my regular widow connections), I mentioned that I was having surgery and my pastor son and wife would be checking on me. With no hesitation, she said, "I'm between homes. Your kids are so busy. How about letting me come to your home to be with you?" She was a perfect "nurse." Knew just where everything was as she cooked, was not suffocating and sensed what I needed when I needed it. I was the recipient of her abounding in God's grace. "We know God is able to make all grace abound to you so that at all times, in all ways, having all that you need, you will abound in grace to others" (2 Cor. 9:8). I'm not good at allowing people to help me, but I'm so glad I said yes.

Gayle is a beautiful decorator and uses that talent for others. Even though she had to move to another state, sell her home, and work full time, she reached out to others by making centerpieces for church events and helping people decorate their homes. "Having projects," she confesses, "keeps me positive and focused." Teresa expressed the same sentiments as she continued her stamping business and sent out cards of encouragement to others. Susie's late husband had left her comfortable financially; therefore, her ministry has been to mentor her grandchildren and help them with college. She often lamented to me that she wanted to have a more definite ministry like teaching Sunday school or working in a shelter. God helped me to convince her that her investment in the lives of her grandchildren was the greatest of ministries. She has taken them on several mission trips where one of her grandsons fell in love with a Spanish speaking country and is now fluent in Spanish and has just secured his first teaching job. When a traumatic event happened in the extended family, Susie's prayer ministry and deep faith brought healing and a new direction.

Before Rod became so ill with cancer that he was in and out of the hospital at least once per month, Lori faithfully taught her class of children at church. After he died, she discovered that she no longer had the stamina, emotionally or physically to continue. As she shared with me, I encouraged her to concentrate on her gardening and wait on God to show her other ministries. Little by little, He has opened opportunities for helping other widows, organizing ladies' ministries and spending more time with her youngest daughter with whom she had been somewhat estranged. On Sundays, the children still come running for a hug, but she is resting and seeking God's will. Who knows what God might have in store? Rod has only been gone for two years.

Kim was one of those young ambitious widows who signed up for too many ministries. The church needed a wedding coordinator. She had the skills and personality and did an amazing job. Being a nurse and loving children, she also volunteered for all the summer church camps. Pretty soon, though, she began to realize that being at weddings was extremely difficult. Working full time as a nurse and caring for her two teens was quite enough to handle for the time being. As she stepped back and listened to God's leading, she realized that her job as a nurse was a big part of her ministry. She helps people who are on disability to rehabilitate in order to go back to work. Yes, she did that before her husband died, but now she had all the childcare and household responsibilities to do alone. God confirmed to her that her nursing gifts were the only ministry she needed right then. A few years later, as her children have graduated from college and gotten married, she has been able to minister to young ladies in a weekly Bible study and continues to invest in the lives of her adult children and their young children. As we walk and talk often, she tells me, "I'm so glad I did not allow other people to make me feel guilty for saying 'no' to some ministries in order to say 'yes' to His perfect plan."

Marcie was only twenty-six when her husband was killed in a trucking accident. She explains that reaching out was hard for her, especially with a two-year-old. She found a Facebook group for young widows and later developed her own blog. Going back to school to become a Spanish teacher has and will continue to bring many opportunities to minister to others. She was a great witness to God's strength as she completed many home projects that she and her husband had begun together.

Beverly Hill McKinney writes an article in a Christian women's magazine that tells of a ministry to widows. When she was at the mall one day, she saw a single lady with whom she struck up a conversation. They exchanged numbers and she realized, "That event helped her see that being alone gives people opportunities to do more, give more, expand more, think deeper, and grow stronger in the Lord."

She went on to begin a ministry of sending cards and organizing social events. As she expresses, "I want other women to know that where they are is not where they will always be."

When Trudy lost her husband, she had to sell their huge home in the mountains. Moving to a new town forced her to find a different church and make new friends. For six years now, she has witnessed to her neighbor, Gloria, who has an ungodly husband and a terminally ill daughter. She and Trudy go shopping together and out to lunch where Trudy has gently talked to her about depending on Jesus to help her. Although Trudy has moved to a different neighborhood, she and Gloria still meet weekly, and now Trudy has started a group of neighborhood women who meet weekly in her home. Gloria often asks for prayer and is reading a great devotional book that Trudy gave her for her birthday.

Keeping the balance between helping others and taking care of your own needs can be an arduous undertaking. The last thing I desired was to wallow in self-pity; however, I learned that I could become irritable and ineffective if I did not work through my own mental and physical needs. Journaling has been one of my greatest tools. Sometimes I don't really know how I feel or the direction God would have me go until I see my thoughts in writing. In the beginning of a widow's grief journey, she often finds it almost impossible to spend that quiet time listening for God's direction or even just knowing He is there to comfort and strengthen. Some widows say they just can't pray. Could it be they just don't have what they feel are the right words? Our definitions of prayer can be so skewed. Prayer is simply being with God, sitting in quietness with maybe some worship music, looking around at creation, thanking, writing or saying God's promises, listening, singing (even when we don't feel like it), thanking, questioning, crying. When I don't feel like doing these things, I cry out to the Lord to help me to just do one thing. Refer to the "Depression Zappers" in chapter 6.

In his booklets on grieving, Steven Hauck tells us that struggling with prayer does not mean we are bad Christians. It's a normal process that may be only temporary. He gives the following suggestions:

- Try arrow prayers. These are small and shot up whenever you can muster the energy.
- Write your prayers—perhaps in a letter form.
- Get others to pray for you.
- Be totally honest with God. Shout out to Him or cry quietly
- Just be in God's presence. Don't worry about what to say. Whatever thoughts bubble up, just present them to God.

Philip Yancy, in his book *Disappointment with God*, points out, "One bold message in the Book of Job is that you can say anything to God. Throw at him your grief, your anger, your doubt, your bitterness, your betrayal, your disappointment—he can absorb them all." Sometimes, we just need to sleep and eat as the prophet Elijah did as told in 1 Kings 18. After ministering in a way that he thought God wanted and seeing great victories, Queen Jezebel threatened his life. He became discouraged and ran and hid. That's okay. He hid in a cave and slept. Then God sent an angel to bring him food and water. Then he slept some more. The bottom line is, God will lead you in whatever ways He knows will be good for you and He will do it in His time and in His way. Don't give up! Take the next step no matter how small.

Suggestions for Ministering to Others

1. Take time to grieve. "Not grieving" is like not bleeding when you are cut.
2. Restore your physical and spiritual soul.
3. Don't do something just because others think you should.
4. Listen and look for God's direction.
5. When possible, confide in a good friend.
6. Make a list of possible ministries that might interest you.
7. Start small such as calling another widow or taking food to a shut in.
8. In your beginning grief journey, you might want to take a leave of absence.

9

Relating to Adult Children and Grandchildren

Papa always did so many fun things like fishing and playing cars with our five grandsons. Even when he was on his deathbed, one of the little guys asked Papa when he could get up to build another race track to zoom their little match box cars down. How could I do that and cook, clean, and do crafts too? The summer right after Doug's passing, we were all at the lake on our church camp ground. I had of course packed all the food, swim toys, sand toys, and towels. The seven- and five-year-old wanted to fish like they always had done with Papa. Not only did I not have the energy, the thought of pulling in one of those scaly little creatures horrified me. As I walked past the pier, I realized God was taking care of the situation. My oldest son had all the fishing gear and was patiently showing his son and their cousins how to bait the hook. Looking back, I realize that must have been difficult for my son since he and his dad had just been fishing on that pier a year before.

Little by little, God showed me that He was present, yet I still felt so empty and inadequate when around the family. I knew my sons were missing their dad, but I was so wrapped up in how they should comfort me that I forgot how they were hurting. Each had a different relationship. My oldest pastor son had that mentor/dad connection. They could sit for hours discussing theology and leadership. Doug was my middle son's sports partner. They knew all the teams and their scores and could be heard for a block away cheering for their teams. Doug loved attending all of my youngest son's musical events. He even took vacation time to attend a huge event that happened on Sunday. (Some people think that is the only day a pastor works.) After the two older boys went to college, Doug found that our youngest son was a deep thinker and a great conversationalist. As the Holy Spirit began to remind me of all these things, God showed me that I needed to be more concerned about their feelings and grief journeys. In his book, *The Death of a Parent*, Delle Chaatman writes,

> Each individual child has a unique perspective on each parent, and that perspective shifts from day to day, age to age, through the giving and taking, through the rebellions and the blissful coming-together times. So—even among us who knew him all our lives—the hole our father's departure has left in our hearts has a different shape, size and depth.

The first thing I realized was that I could not expect my adult sons to understand my grief. Yes, my middle son has lost his young wife to cancer, but he had two children and a host of support from his in-laws. He had remarried by this time also. None of my sons had known a love of forty-six years. I lost my dad when I was a child whereas they had a much longer and richer time with their dad. My sons and their dad were so close in their own ways. No wonder they were so empty and did not know how to comfort me.

My oldest son seemed to have the greatest bond with his dad. On one of Doug's last days, he told my son, "Get everyone to come. I'm going now." Jeff called us all up to the hospital room. About that time, Doug awoke and as Jeff bent his six-foot-two frame down to Doug's ear, he heard, "Jeff, why am I still here? I thought I would be in Heaven." Jeff, tenderly and with tears responded, "Dad, you have to wait your turn. God is not quite ready." My sons were doing their absolute best, and as I began to understand their grief more, God brought the comfort I needed in other ways such as books and friends. With each year, I sensed my sons' loving and understanding toward me as I gave them time to work through their own grief. I also realized as I looked back that I had not been the perfect comforter for my mother when she lost her second and third husbands.

Two years after Doug passed, I was visiting in my middle son's home. As he and his dad had often done on Saturday afternoons, he was watching football. Knowing I was too sleepy to drive the four hours home to Michigan, I sat/lay down on the couch where he was sitting/standing and yelling for his team. While making a few comments about his team, I drifted in and out of sleep. Truly, I was not watching the game. As the game ended and I awoke, Vince exclaimed, "Wow, Mom? Thanks for watching the game with me. It kind of felt like part of Dad was here watching with me." Boy, was I glad I needed a nap before traveling. By this time, the little boys were awake from their naps. Their dad even told them that Gramma watched the game with him.

What a challenge to get ready for all five grandsons and their parents to come for the holidays. Holidays are difficult anyway, but to do it alone was overwhelming. Since I did not want to be exhausted when they arrived, I prepared many freezer meals and had a friend come over to help me set up all the beds. My two youngest love all the school toys and games in my basement so I had to get them all organized. (At least I thought I did.) Wrapping gifts, baking, church work! I truly wondered how I could do it without Doug. One of the first things I had to do was to delegate more…just wait until they arrived and have them make the beds. Assign each family a meal to prepare and clean up after. Assign tasks such as grocery shopping to each family. Even with all that, I still found myself exhausted after they left. Grief will do that to a person who is normally full of energy.

The first holiday season found me still washing sheets and put-ting things away three weeks later. My older grandsons did help carry all the sheets and towels to the laundry room, but of course, they had to leave as I began to wash. My other family was already on their way to her parents' home in West Virginia. As I asked the Lord to help me, I realized that no one really cared when I got the sheets and towels washed, and I thought about when my daughter-in-law would return the next week. I had not thought to ask, and she had not thought to offer. She was delighted when I told her they were invited to come for pizza when they got home and we would put everything away. Guess what? The toys were in a mess again. What is one week in the scheme of things anyway?

Two years after Doug passed, our last grandson was born in Cleveland, Ohio. Driving there alone, I remembered how we had been together for each of the other four. Oh, the excitement we shared as we arrived at the hospital for the first one born nine hours away from our home in Kentucky. Would we make it? How would it be to take turns holding him? The next one was born in Tennessee, and then we even got to fly to Ireland to welcome the third one. Our fourth grandson was born right here in Michigan. Now, I was to welcome the fifth little guy...alone. I was praising God for four hours of travel safety from Kalamazoo, Michigan, to Cleveland, Ohio. Still, I had this indescribable feeling of lostness. Both of the other grandparents were there, which made it even more evident to me that I was alone. God helped me to find my way through that huge hospital to the room where everyone was rejoicing at this new birth. I began to feel God's presence and strength surge through my mind and body as God brought to my mind Romans 8:26, "The Spirit helps us in our weakness."

When my son and his wife took little Bennett home, I was to stay in their home to help care for the older toddler brother, cook for the two teen sons, and take them to needed school events. Being directionally challenged and with no GPS, I constantly sent up SOS prayers. My teen grandsons would try to direct me; however, they often told me about a turn a little too late to move over in the traffic. My mind was probably a little fuzzy since I had been up in the night with the baby. Spending the night in the home of one of your adult children's home without your spouse can be a traumatic experience. Who would take a turn changing a diaper, listen for that little newborn cry, collaborate over strategies for care, not only of the baby, but the two teen age sons? I definitely was not up to the task. I kept

111

repeating the verse from Isaiah 54:5. "God is my husband." I would just talk aloud, "Okay, God, I need you now." Then His strength would sweep over me. With God's amazing grace, I was able to meet the challenges and enjoy the family.

Kim traveled all the way to Germany to meet her first grandchild. Later, her daughter and family moved back to the States and moved in with her until they could get adjusted. Another grandchild joined the family which made for a full house. Of course, Kim loved having them close; however, her son-in-law thought she needed help with certain decisions. Kim, in her kind and loving way assured her family that they were welcome, but she was capable of making major decisions such as which car to drive and repairs on the home. Sometimes we widows forget that we are the head of the home and have those rights and responsibilities. With prayer and communication, her daughter's family and she have a wonderful relationship. They moved into their own home and Kim sold the large house and purchased a condo. Her son-in-law adores her and often just shows up with flowers and even takes her on a "date" dinner. Kim loves helping with the grandchildren even though sometimes her adult children think she is incorrigible and can work full time during the week and take care of the grandchildren on the weekend. Kim has learned to set boundaries and choose special times for each grandchild to come for that special weekend with Gramma.

One of my grandsons (the one who wanted Papa to get up and play cars with him) lives in the same city as I do. He could already read when he entered kindergarten, but as he progressed to second grade, he struggled with math and writing. Gramma's help was surely needed to pick him up from school two afternoons a week to finish homework. At times, his parents needed a break on the weekend so Jackson stayed with me. We cooked together, watched documentaries on YouTube, read stories from *Readers' Digest*, played games, and read Bible stories before bed. Even at age twelve, he still loves to watch *Wheel of Fortune* and *Jeopardy*. (He sometimes gets more correct answers than I do.) He loves to hear stories about Papa and his own dad growing up. Helping him and teaching classes at church helped with my grief of no longer being a classroom teacher. In recent years,

I've grown more accustomed to traveling alone to visit my grandsons in Ohio. On the five-hour drive, I listen to music and books, pray and memorize scripture...sometimes catch up on phone calls. My comfort level in staying in my children's home has improved. It is still hard to go to my room at night alone. I always try to have a great book to read and, of course, music on my phone.

On one occasion, I stayed with the five- and three-year-olds while their older brothers and parents went to a general convention for our church denomination. My daughter-in-law left all the emergency numbers and other instructions, but I still felt a little anxious about being there alone with them. Wouldn't you know, the electricity went out the first really warm night? Did I mention, I had to care for the dog also? When she needed to go outside, I had to make sure the little boys were sleeping as I listened on the monitor. During the day, I had to take them with me to walk her. Sure wish Papa had been there to help, but anytime I start to complain, I quote a much-needed verse from Philippians 2:14. "Do all things without complaining." Then I begin to give thanks for all the good things. That's when the victory comes. It's especially easy for a widow to spiral down into a pit of self-pity. One of my favorite authors is Lynn Austin. In her latest book, *If I Were She*, she wrote, "It does no good to sit in the mud and mope. Either get up and wash yourself off or get used to the puddle." I did a lot of "washing" that week, but overall, I gave thanks that I could be there. Did I mention that I was allergic to the dog and my eyes swelled almost shut?

Another way, God helped me to feel needed was when this family of six went to the beach for the day. Everyone was in the water except the nineteen-year-old and me. He began to ask questions about when his papa and I fell in love, like "How did you know? Do you think an eighteen-year-old can fall in love...? It was surely a "God moment." I'm so thankful for the confidence and trust that he had to talk to me. Must have been all those games we played, traveling to and from Lacrosse games, and practicing driving in the cemetery when his parents didn't have time. This past Christmas break from college where he is a sophomore, he brought that beautiful, now twenty-year-old, to my home in Michigan. We played more games, baked cookies, and talked about their future. She is a junior studying criminal justice and he is a studying to be a youth pastor. Their goal is to finish college before marriage. When I asked her what she loved about my grandson, she quickly responded with, "I love the way he cares about others and always wants to help." I didn't mention that Doug and I got married after our sophomore years.

Since Teresa suffered from a lung disease, her daughter, a nurse, decided to move back to the States and live in their mom's home. At first, that seemed like a great arrangement until Teresa began to feel like a prisoner in her own home. Her daughter told her when she could run the washer and how to walk on the upper level so as to not disturb the children's nap time. She was also admonished not to correct or redirect the children when they misbehaved. This would be quite a challenge for a former primary teacher of thirty years. Talking about Jesus was not permitted. Teresa began to realize that having them move in was not a good idea. In her book, *Alone and Alive*, Janet Boyanton, an attorney who lost her husband when her son was only nine years old expresses a warning with these words. "If you decide to allow a person to move in with you, make sure the ground rules are clear." She even suggests that a lawyer draw up a contract. Most widows in their state of shock would not think of doing this with their own son or daughter with whom they have always been so close.

Teresa tried to be considerate; however, her daughter also wanted to go through her dad's things and tell her mom what to keep. She constantly admonished her not to spend any money even though Rick had left her with more than adequate life insurance and other assets. They finally had to resort to a meeting with their pastor. Thankfully, she was able to stand her ground and ask her children to find a different home. When they did, Teresa was never invited to their home for even a birthday celebration for the grandchildren. With much prayer and counseling, the family has come back together after four years. Teresa's other daughter has really struggled on her grief journey, which called for Teresa to spend much time listening and guiding. Moms do that! Never mind her own grief. Her granddaughter suffers from depression and has tried to commit suicide several times. Life goes on. Traumatic situations still happen, God is always with us. "God is our refuge and strength, a very present help in trouble" (Ps. 46:1).

Amy has a good relationship with her daughters, but once again, she wound up comforting them when she needed comfort. Frustration sets in when they wait until the last minute to plan family events and inform their mom when and where...sometimes at the last minute. Amy has always been the planner and organizer and now she has to wait around to see what they want to do. Giving thanks is her strategy to keep things moving. Over the past few years, she has learned that a good relationship is more important than when or where a celebration is being held. She continually gives her girls a break to go on dates with their husbands and friends. Her grandchildren were so close to their grandpa. When he was sick, the eight-year-old girl would climb into his bed with him and hug him. After he died, the older boy did not want to sleep in the room where Grandpa had died. Gramma had to comfort that grandson even though her own heart was heavy.

Marcia experiences stress when disciplining her two-year-old. She reports there is no back up, and she feels like the "bad guy." Since her young husband's death, her own family wants to indulge the grandson and offer little help. She has begun to date again but finds it so much more challenging to find child care. Her little guy cries when she leaves. Maybe he thinks she might not come back like Daddy. I'm pretty sure Marcia has everything under control when I see pictures of her now four-year-old son with her at Disney World. Yes, she drove with him there all by herself. What a brave and feisty lady she has become!

Mary has a wonderful family who always went on vacation together when Jack was alive. They decided to do so the next year after he died. Mary called me when they got back home to express her struggle to be there without Jack. Going to her room at night alone and not having anyone with whom to debrief when the families had a conflict was devastating to her. As we talked and prayed, she realized what a struggle they were having without Dad. They could not possibly understand what it's like to lose a spouse. They love their mom and just don't expect her to be sad. She had always been the peppy, positive, and fun loving one. Over the last seven years, they have often invited her to their homes. Her daughter lives only an hour away and is super busy with a full-time job, singing and playing in the praise band at church, and transporting three teens to their various activities. Mary does not "sit in the mud puddle and mope." She graciously goes once a week to help her daughter with projects. Even though she hates to fly, she does so in order to see her son and family. They do not realize how hurtful it can be for them to be sitting around in the living room all on their cell phones. They do love her very much, but just think Mom is okay. Should she tell them? Only discernment from God can let her know what to do.

Surely our adult children do not realize our feelings since they have not been through any of these things. They are busy with their own families but will begin to understand as their own children mature. Trudy has three adult children and five grandchildren. Her son suffers from depression and never calls his mom. They even moved 800 miles away from where they lived one mile from their mom. She only found out via Facebook. Her daughter went through a divorce and turned her back on her faith. She refuses any contact with her mom. Thankfully, the other daughter shows her devotion by calling her every day from wherever she is as a flight attendant. Trudy has been faithfully sending cards and texts as she prays for her children and grandchildren. Just this past few months, her oldest daughter has rededicated her life to God. Her estranged son has been sending texts telling of his love for her and the other daughter has remarried and seems to be turning back to God. Trudy continues to stand by the words of the prophet, Jeremiah in chapter 32:17. "Ah sovereign Lord, you have made the heavens and the earth with your great power and outstretched arm. Nothing is too hard for you."

God works in His way and in His time. Trudy had kept up her relationship with the grandchildren as much as possible by sending cards and making phone calls. When one of her teenage grandsons got a job at a local grocery store, she would just pop in to see him. As he began to mature and fell in love, he wanted grandma at his wedding, thus bringing his dad and grandma together. Trudy's granddaughter whose mom had turned her back on God recently got married and wanted Trudy to come. Once again, God has a way of bringing reconciliation. Trudy reports how happy she is that she did not give up. She kept sending those cards and gifts to show her love.

Pastor and clinical psychologist, Dr. Kenneth C. Haugk gives insight concerning how adult children might be feeling when their parent dies.

> Deep inside we often assume your parents will always be there. If our other parent is still alive, we may be so concerned about them that we forget about our own grief. If we are left with no parents, we may begin to think about our own mortality. One man said, "My dad was the last one left in our family from his generation. When he died, I felt I was next."

Trudy's oldest son, who has suffered depression even before his dad died might have been experiencing this feeling. My oldest son was overly concerned about my living alone, especially when I had the heart issues. Perhaps, he even put his own grief on the back burner. In recent years, I have apologized to him for not understanding his grief. With tears in his eyes, he told me that he had seen a therapist to help him. Over these past years, I think all of my sons have seen that God has truly given me strength to feel whole again. When Doug was alive I would often express that I was a "kept woman." Now I exclaim that I am a "blessed woman." My sons and I understand each other's grief much better.

In her wonderful book, *When People Grieve*, Paula D'Arcy writes about losing her mother. She had already lost her young husband and a child, but losing a parent was different. Her words after the funeral were "In the days that followed, I repeatedly felt as if a great tide had come to pull me into deeper waters and that my mother was no longer there to obscure that greater reality… Everything was shifting. I felt as if I had formerly been tethered to a mooring and now the holding me to the dock had been untied, propelling me into new seas.

I had to let go and let my grief take me to new places." I have seen this happening in the lives of all of my sons. My oldest has become even deeper in his prayer life and realizes that his Dad left him a great legacy that inspires him to be a better husband, father, and pastor. His feelings of anger while attending a special church service as he asked, "Why did God take my dad?" have changed to "God let my dad come home." My middle son recently expressed to me that he thought his dad would be so proud because in his new job, they call him Pastor Vince. He is a staff member who does all of the media for a large church in Ohio. My youngest son is still struggling, but I cling to Psalm 77:14. "You are the God who performs miracles."

I have heard more than one widow say that they felt the wrong parent died. I wouldn't go that far, but I could see how difficult it was for my sons to lose their dad's prayer support, listening ear, confident, sports partners, spiritual guide, steady and strong friend, a grandfather for their own sons, and much more. My heart hurt for them. I just could not do some of those things. As I sought wisdom, God showed me that I could encourage them in their jobs and families by watching their children and helping my pastor son with some "behind the scenes" church activities and most of all, praying for them. I have been able to cook dinner for one of the families once per week and enjoy a game time. At first, I thought I had to do everything to fill in that hole their dad left, but I realized that I don't have to "be doing" so much. I just have "to be." I can be their greatest fan. I can be their prayer support. I can be the person who loves them. I rest in the words of Isaiah 44:3b–4. "I will pour out my Spirit on your offspring, and my blessings on your descendants. They will spring up like grass in a meadow."

Sometimes when our lives change, our adult children are not so sure about our new adventures such as dating. When Kim began dating, her thirty-year-old daughter told her she could not get married a second time because she, herself, had not been married once. (She is now.) When things really began to get serious with Kim and her fiancé, both daughters and even many of the relatives gave all kinds of advice. "Do you really know this guy?" Where will you live?" "How will you separate the finances?" Of course they knew their mom had always been a woman of prayer and wisdom; however, their immediate reactions did not indicate that. One of the daughters even expressed the sentiment that if Mom remarried, it was like putting the final nail in her dad's coffin. At first, Kim was really hurt. How could they understand? They had not been alone for twelve years taking care of young daughters while working full time as a nurse and managing a household. Thankfully, she did not say anything as she prayed for wisdom and patience. Her daughters have come to appreciate their mom's fiancé and will all rejoice as she remarries in a few weeks. He is a wonderful man who loves to help with home projects. I told her that since they will be living just down the street to remember that I'm her close friend.

Keeping those strong ties with and among our adult children and grandchildren can be a challenge; however, the results are worth it. Some think the widow has enough on her plate so why does she have to make such an effort? Shouldn't her friends, children, and other relatives reach out to her more often? Perhaps, but we are all on our own journeys. Paula D'Arcy sums it up with these words. "When navigating the waters of grief, you don't prevail by opposing them. You prevail by surrendering to grief's wisdom. You agree to stand undefended before things that are not permanent and let pain pull you toward everything that lasts."

Suggestions for Relating to Adult and Grandchildren

1. Try to be rested before going to their homes so you can be more patient.
2. Take a good book or music for the time you go into your room alone.
3. Listen and try to understand their grief journey.
4. Realize that they have not walked in your shoes.
5. Send cards, games, and books to young grandchildren.
6. Send cookies, encouragement cards or texts, and money to college students.
7. FaceTime them often.
8. If you live close enough, go their school games and other activities.
9. Above all, pray for each one.

10

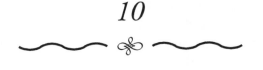

Knowing Who I Am and How Much Stronger I Am

First of all, I know that even though I am no longer a wife, a pastor's wife, or a classroom teacher, I am a mom, a gramma, and best of all, a child of God. Romans 8:15 tells me, "You should not behave like cowering, fearful slaves. You should behave instead as God's own child, adopted into his family, calling him Abba, Father. For it is his spirit deep within that tells us we are His children" (Rom. 8:15 NLT). I can talk to the God of the universe anytime, anywhere. He is always with me. Each year, my confidence grows as a single person. I even love some things about being single such as

- sleeping and eating when I want,
- choosing foods that I like and my husband didn't,
- going places anytime I want,
- watching movies or listening to music of my choice when I choose,
- singing at the top of my lungs in my house or car,
- trying new hobbies.

You might be asking, "Couldn't you do those things before?" Yes, but we sometimes differed. He never denied my cooking certain things. I just wanted to please him. Sometimes when I'm at the grocery store, I look at the Brussel sprouts and think, "I won't get those because Doug doesn't like them." Then I remind myself, "I will because I do like Brussel sprouts."

Over the past eight years, I have tried several new things such as learning to play the flute. Too much work, but fun. I love playing my high school instrument, the cornet, in a community college band two days per week. One of my dreams was to teach on the college level. I kept telling myself that I was too old and the students wouldn't relate to me. One day as I was sitting in my "prayer chair," I suddenly felt inspired to update my resume and write a cover letter to a local university. These things usually take me a long time, but I whipped up the documents in about an hour and sent them in. I knew I wanted to teach entry level courses in reading or strategies for teachers, but I didn't know a contact person. After praying for wisdom and direction, I called the information desk at the university. Since it was a holiday, the student receptionist answered and gave me all the information that I needed. I sent my resume and cover letter via email. Two days later, to my utter surprise, I received a call from the head of the Literacy Department asking when I would like to come for an interview.

I continued to be surprised as I talked with the head of the department. I was thinking, *She acts like the position is mine if I want it. I'm not even sure I can do it. Now, we all know adjunct professors don't make much money. Maybe they are desperate.* They weren't and I did take the position, thinking, "God has led me this far and He will direct my path. Wow! Did I ever need help with the technology! I felt proud as I figured out how to use the monitors, DVD player, overhead machine, etc., in the classroom. Of course, I went early each time to make sure everything was working. It always did until the day my supervisor came for an observation. I sent up another SOS prayer and all went well. Then it came time to figure out the grading system. Not having Doug to encourage and help me brought many tears. While tossing and turning in bed one night, a light came on in my head about which keys to push. Success! Praise God! Another miracle. I was learning to trust and receive God's grace little by little. "His strength was surely evident in my weakness" (2 Cor. 12:9).

Due to the COVID-19 pandemic, all part time professors and some of the full time were let go. What would I do now? I loved the structure of part time work and the extra money was an added blessing. Later that week, I saw an ad for Census enumerators that paid well and had flexible hours. Even though I would have to wear a mask and drive all over my area, I applied and was accepted. One of my sons didn't want me to and the other two thought I would enjoy it. I did, and felt safe the whole time. I met many interesting people and hopefully brought a smile to many of their faces. Yes, there were a few moments, but God kept me safe and positive. Second Thessalonians 3:3 assures me. "But the Lord is faithful, and he will strengthen and protect you."

Making decisions in a more timely manner is more evidence of progress in my grief journey. In our marriage, I was the encourager and planner, but Doug was great at making decisions. When he first died, I purchased a new table for the living room and returned two before I made the right decision. After teaching at the university, I chose a whole new living room set and was able to pay cash for it. With my census money, I have selected and made the choice for a new oven. Talking to myself helps. "Paula, you are a mature, well-educated person. You can research all the best appliances and make a choice." As the store delivered and installed my new stove, I thought, "Look at that, Doug. I know you are proud that I did this all by myself." More assurance of God's grace.

I am still a teacher for a ladies' Bible study, my grandsons, and my sons. One advantage is that I choose my classes, and I have all the study time I need. I talk to God a lot more than I used to. Oh, I thought I was "quite spiritual" when Doug was alive. I found out just how weak I was and how much I needed to depend on God. After rereading the chapter in this book about ways to relate to my grandsons, I realize even more how valuable that role is. Now that two of them are becoming adults, they seem to enjoy talking with me about college events, dating, life goals, and ways to relate to their parents. Recently, when my youngest son, their uncle was very ill at my home, one of them called two times to check and ask if he could help. He was in a town close by playing in a lacrosse tournament. I was supposed to go watch the game, but my grandson was so understanding and thinking of others. I expressed my appreciation and that he should not come due to his uncle's being contagious.

Lori has spent many hours in the last year and one-half crying because her adult children refuse to come to her house. They make up excuses like "There is nothing to do because you don't have cable. We don't want to be where we witnessed our dad in so much pain." Her children have indicated that she is not as educated as they are and is a "dinosaur thinker." Wonder where they think they got their intelligence and who sent them to college. How did she manage three children while her husband was out of town for weeks at a time? How did she take courses to become a master gardener? She has made new friends through her church and found people to help her completely remodel her home. She sends pictures to her children hoping that they will come, but they just say it's good that she has help.

Her love of God, reading the scriptures, and praying have all kept her positive and moving forward. When I talked with her on the phone a few weeks ago, she was praising God for his provision. She needed a wall in her house removed. She just mentioned it to a young man who was shopping for tools. He came by the next week and said, "I have some extra time this week and can remove that wall." All he wanted was a keyboard that he had seen in her storage area. Lori is realizing that God is her strength, and she is standing firm in her faith. Although Lori is sad, she is moving forward. We are praying and believing that her children will begin to realize this and develop a faith of their own.

Suzie was left with making huge financial decisions. Maybe you are thinking, *I wish I had more finances to make decisions about.* Since her late husband had handled all the details, she was feeling overwhelmed but was not crippled to the point of not being able to move forward. She relied heavily on God's wisdom and direction as she found a Christian financial advisor. Together, they set up ways to share the money. She, of course, supports her church, has been able to help her pastor son, missions, college tuition for her grandchildren, and Christian programs on TV and radio, all the while remaining the fun friend who likes to find bargains as we shop together. She lives in a modest and tastefully decorated home where she offers hospitality on a regular basis. Since the time of her husband's death she has continued to be faithful to God, her family, and friends. Although she did not have a goal to date anyway, recently God has brought a man into her life. Suzie is not sure how things will progress, but continues to be involved in prayer ministry, playing tennis, and witnessing to her neighbors.

One of my most beautiful and talented widow friends, Gayle, has been a widow for over twenty years. After finally meeting her soul mate, they had only seven wonderful years. She was left with huge financial burdens and a breakdown in family ties due to her dad's estate. After lovingly caring for her dad with help from her loving husband, her family felt that she made the wrong choices about his care. In his beginning stages of dementia, he had become somewhat violent, so Gayle had to take some action that her extended family found fault. Not only was she grieving the loss of her husband, she had no support or encouragement from family. Being one of the greatest prayer warriors I know, she did not allow these circumstances to defeat her. Oh, I'm sure she might have felt like the prophet, Elijah at times, wanting to sit under an old broom tree and ask God to let her die, but she did what God told Elijah to do...pray and wait on the Lord. See 1 Kings 19. She was able to get their beautiful home on a lake ready for sale even though she had to sell it at a loss. She had to move in with her son for a while but kept ministering and working full time. Over the past twenty years, she has worked five different jobs and moved five times. She has been in the same place now for six years and continues to minister in her church and to her neighbors. She just began a neighborhood Bible study a few weeks ago. Her courage and testimony to God's grace are a blessing to all.

After six years of being a widow, Mary continues to realize her gifts of evangelism. She never meets a stranger, and with her sparkly personality and enthusiasm, she tells them about Jesus. On one occasion, visiting her in the Cape Cod area, we were at the beach when two young ladies crowded in behind us even though there was plenty of room down the beach. At first, I was a little irritated, but the Holy Spirit prompted me that God was probably arranging a time for Mary to share. When we were getting ready to leave, I asked one of the girls, Jane, to take our picture. She began to tell us how grateful she was that we made room for them behind us. (Thankfully, she didn't pick up on my first thoughts.) And that, of course, she would love to take our picture. She asked us how we met, and of course, Joyce began her story of God's leading when my husband and I were her pastors…how her husband truly committed his life to Christ and that's why she was sure she would meet him in heaven someday. Jane began to tell us that she had given up on God because of the death of her husband and all the problems with her family arguing over the estate.

We told her that God had surely not given up on her because that morning we had prayed that God would lead us to someone who needed to know His love. Mary always carries copies of the devotional book, *Jesus Calling*, by Sarah Young. She asked Jane if she would mind if she went to her car to get a copy. When Mary returned carrying the book, Jane exclaimed, "Oh my gracious!" (Actually more colorful words.) When Mary asked her if she had read it, she said, "No, but I think I should since my sister just bought me a copy. We left the beach thinking we might never see Jane again and praying that she would find her way. Two weeks late, Mary was in one of the many small shopping areas when guess who walked by. Yes, Jane and she were able to reconnect, which is a true miracle since they did not have each other's numbers or addresses and the Cape Cod area is so populated. God is truly using Mary to bring other to him and although she still misses her husband, she continues to move forward.

Widowed at twenty-six with a young son to care for, Marcie has struggled to continue her education and become a Spanish teacher. Of course she would rather have her sweet husband, but she tells of following her dream and continuing her education with God's help. After two years, she has begun to date; however, she explains how much more challenging it is with being a single mom and going to school. Her story to move forward and realize the grace and strength God gives is surely an inspiration to all.

Teresa knew she was making progress in her grief journey when she went to Florida without Rick. She was able to make decisions about their former living quarters and eventually purchased a new home. There she attended a "Grief Share" group. As she went through the workbook and the sessions, she began to realize everything they suggested, she had already done. God had been her grief counselor. Even though one of her children has been belligerent and uncooperative, she has kept praying and seeking God's direction. They are now doing much better. As Shelia Walsh writes in her book, *It's Okay Not to Be Okay*, states, "The grief journey is not a sprint, but a marathon." Many times widows hear the unwelcome words, "Time will heal." There is of course an element of truth in that, but as you can see from these brave widow's stories, we take action during that waiting. We know God is our husband, and He gives wisdom and grace to move forward and keep on becoming the person he has created us to be.

After Kim's young husband died suddenly, she was left with working a full-time job as a nurse, meeting the needs of her college age daughter who suffers from anxiety and having her other daughter living oversees with her military husband. After facing the immediate devastation, she began to realize she was making progress as her family gave support. In the beginning of her grief journey, Kim wanted to keep being involved in the ministry for her church as a wedding coordinator. Members of the family and church thought all those tears were her being happy for the bliss shared by the newlyweds. Her pastor began to notice and talked to her about letting that ministry go and since her gift is hospitality, he asked if she would open her home for a young women's Bible study...not facilitate, just be there. Over the last nine years, she has grown with that group and realizes how God has built her confidence. She is even dating again. Yes, she met him online through a Christian site. Now, we know those aren't always what they are cracked up to be, but Kim is a woman of prayer and Bible study. As I talk with her on our many three-mile walks, I have no doubt that she will make the right decision.

While on vacation in Myrtle Beach with a widow friend and two couples, we decided to try parasailing. On the boat that took us out, we met a middle age newly married couple. As we talked, she told us that she was widowed for several years. Her young husband, a pastor, had passed when they were in their twenties. She described how terrified she was to move on, but stepped out to go back to school to be a flight attendant. While she was doing that, she took more classes and became a grief counselor. At her forty-fifth high school reunion, she met a man who had lived in the same town but attended a different high school. He was a radio broadcaster and a university professor. They fell in love and were on their honeymoon. God is good to send us stories like this to encourage us. If she can do all that, I can move on too.

A few years after Doug passed, I noticed that I would see couples at the mall holding hands and my attitude had changed. I actually felt happy for them rather than so sad that I didn't have anyone. Sometimes, I would stop to chat with them and tell them how sweet they looked. I would tell them that I loved the way they seemed to love each other and how thankful I was for the forty-seven years I got to do that. When at the grocery store, I would remind ladies how blessed they were to have their husbands to help pack and carry the groceries. When I go grocery shopping now, I try to always tell the clerk what a good job they are doing and especially if they have someone bagging. That's another way I know I'm doing better. I feel more thankful for those around me and empathize for those ladies who are alone.

Over these past few years, I sleep better and have more energy to reach out to others. Reading and studying God's word has become more exciting and I actually remember what I've read. In the past few months, I have reread many of the books on grief that I read when Doug first passed. I have a whole new perspective and a feeling of growth. They just make more sense. I've realized that sometimes I have to hurt before I can heal. None of those tears went to waste. Greif tore away many things that were not that important and to allow me to see who I really am. I am free to set new goals and with all God's energy that works in me to continue on this exciting journey called "life." Reminders of Doug have turned from deep sadness to cherished memories and thankfulness.

I've learned so much about myself. When Doug was alive, I leaned more on him than I did God. Oh, I didn't realize it until I lost him, but the ugly truth stared me in the face when I had to make decisions such as securing a home equity loan and then how to use the funds. Courage is not doing things we don't fear. As John Wayne once expressed, "Courage is being afraid and saddling up anyway." Mistakes are okay. We learn and go on. When the tasks are completed or the decision made, we feel more confident. Of course, mistakes are made, but now I tend to look at them as learning experiences. That's just one more miracle of God's grace.

In the beginning of my grief journey, I learned that I was not as much of an extrovert as I had thought. Sure, there were many times when Doug was busy talking with others at social events, but I knew he was there, and he would be taking me home where we would collaborate. Now, as I leave church or another social gathering, I think about each contact I have made and give thanks for them. If no one invites me to sit at their table at a church dinner, I look around for another single person or couples I love to be with and boldly ask if I may sit with them. Haven't been turned down yet!

On this journey, I've found myself asking, "Were you pleasant and patient in your own strength or was it just because you had Doug who was always encouraging? Can you be positive without that? If not, what kind of Christian are you? Do you allow the Holy Spirit to dwell in you and strengthen you?" I've had to ask for forgiveness and wisdom to rely on God to strengthen me with power through his Spirit in my inner being (Eph. 3:16a). I've learned to have an attitude of expectancy. What will God do next in my life? In the Old Testament, we find Habakkuk crying out for help. He thought God was not coming to his rescue or the rescue of the nation. God answered him with "Look at the nations and watch and be utterly amazed. For I am going to do something in your days that you would not believe, even if you were told" (Hab. 1:5–8). I want to be watching and listening. I have been amazed over and over at God's provision and how many new things I have learned. I'm ready to be amazed again and again.

Janet Boyanton, a lawyer, who lost her husband when her son was only ten years of age, has written a book that truly encapsulates the ideas of a widow's struggles, by her ability to move on. The title says it all. *Alone and Alive.* She reminds us that our husbands died, but we did not. She tells how she began to feel relatively normal again as she recognized that she would survive. She goes on to express how she had gone through the anger, the guilt, the immense sadness, and the years of walking around in a trance. She was just driving down a street lined with trees that were springing forth with leaves and blossoms when she suddenly found herself smiling for no apparent reason. There was no forcing. It just came naturally. She had one of those "aha" moments as she realized that she had not smiled much for a few years.

If you are a new widow, you may be thinking, "I will never get there." There will be days of vacillating between feelings of overwhelming defeat and unshakable determination. Slowly, you will become aware that the determination is winning. Oh, this isn't just gritting your teeth or pulling yourself up by the book straps. It is a dependence on God to help as He has promised to make His strength perfect in our weakness. It is asking for wisdom to set goals. It is walking into our grief and experiencing it so we can heal. It can even be "enjoying the journey." It is setting goals such as the ones Ruth Sissom tells in her book, *Instantly a Widow.*

- Commit my life each morning to the purpose of glorifying Christ.
- Spend time during daily Bible study to apply what I am reading.
- Stay involved in daily routine that brings personal satisfaction.
- Allow others to help me.
- Look for creative ways to use my skills, education, personality, and other resources.

Your goals may be different, but they will give you direction as you continue to make this journey. Paul tells us in Philippians 4:12 and 13, "I have learned the secret of being content in any and every situation. I can do all things through Him who gives me strength." We can see that new thing that God is doing as expressed in Isaiah 43:19, "See, I am doing a new thing. Now, it springs up; do you not perceive it?" We can't move on if we are holding on. We will never go back to our old self. Rather we will become a new person.

Resources

Barranco, Jene Ray. *Good Night, I Love You*. New York: Faith Words, 2017.

Bentz, Joseph. *When God Takes Too Long*. Missouri: Beacon Hill Press, 2005.

Boyaton, Janet. *Alone and Alive*. New Jersey: Shafer Publishing, 2011.

Brecheisen, Jerry and Lawrence W. Wilson. *When Life Doesn't Turn Out the Way You Expect*.
Missouri: Beacon Hill Press, 2003.

Brizendine, Judy. *Stunned by Grief*. California: Bennett Knepp Publishing, 2011.

Fleet, Brody, Carole. *Happily Even After*. California: Cleis Press, Inc., 2012.

Chatman, Delle. *The Death of a Parent*. Illinois: ACTA Publications, 2001.

D'Arcy, Paula. *When People Grieve*. New York: The Crossroads Publishing Co., 2013.

D'Arcy, Paula. *When Your Friend Is Grieving*. Illinois: Harold Shaw Publishers, 1990.

Dunn, Bill and Kathy Leonard. *Through a Season of Grief*. Tennessee: Thomas Nelson, 2004.

Eib, Lynn. *When God and Grief Meet*. Illinois: Tyndale Publishers, 2009.

Extravagant Grace. Michigan: Zondervan Publishing House, 2000.

Ginsburg, M. S., Genevieve Davis. *Widow to Widow*. Massachusetts: DaCapo Life Long Publishers, 1997.

Haugk, Kenneth C. *Journeying Through Grief.* St Louis: Mo: Stephen Ministries, 2004.

Jeremiah, David. *Forward.* Tennessee: W Publishing, an imprint of Thomas Nelson, 2020.

Johnson, Barbara. *Pack Up Your Gloomies in a Great Big Box.* Dallas: Word Publishing, 1993.

Levy, Alexander, *The Orphaned Adult.* Massachusetts: Perseus Books, 1999.

Lewis, C. S. *A Grief Observed.* New York: Bantam Books, 1961.

Nyman, Margaret. *Hope for an Aching Heart.* Michigan: Discovery House Publishers, 2012.

O'Malley, Patrick O., PhD. *Getting Grief Right.* Colorado: Sounds True Publishing, 2017.

Peterson, Lorraine. *Restore My Sout, A Grief Companion.* Colorado: Navpress, 2000.

Ross, Elisabeth Kubler and David Kessler. *On Grief and Grieving.* New York: Scribner, 2005.

Sittser, Gerald L. *A Grace Disguised.* Michigan: Zondervan Publishing House, 1995.

Sisson, Ruth. *Instantly a Widow.* Michigan: Discovery House Publishers, 1990.

Truesdale, Al. *When You Can't Pray.* Missouri: Beacon Hill Press, 2002.

Trent, Tammy. *Learning to Breathe Again.* Tennessee: Thomas Nelson, 2004.

Walsh, Sheila. *It's Okay Not to Be Okay.* Michigan: Baker Books, 2018.

Westberg, Granger E. *Good Grief.* Minneapolis: Fortress Press, 2011.

Williams, Joyce. *Unshakable Faith for Shaky Times.* Missouri: Beacon Hill Press of Kansas City, 2005.

Wiseman, Carol. *Emerging from the Heartache of Loss.* Colorado: Blue Mountain Press, 2013.

Wolfelt, Alan D., PhD. *Healing a Spouse's Grieving Heart.* Colorado: Companion Press, 2003.

Wolfelt, Alan D., PhD. *Healinga the Adult Child's Grieving Heart.* Colorado: Companion Press, 2002.

Wright, Norman H. *Experiencing Grief.* Tennessee: B & H Publishing Group, 2004.

Zonnebelt Smeenge, Susan and Robert C. DeVries. *Getting to the Other Side of Grief.* Michigan: Baker Books, 1998.

About the Author

Paula McVay is a graduate of Southern Nazarene University with degrees in elementary and secondary education. Her master's work was completed at Syracuse University in New York. Being certified in K–12, she has taught at all grade levels, including some adjunct work at Western Michigan University in Kalamazoo, Michigan, where she now resides. Her main focus however was being a mom to three wonderful sons and a gramma to five delightful grandsons. She loved being a pastor's wife and being involved in children's, women's, and music ministry, which always included her children. Although she participated in writing leagues in high school and has had several articles published in an online Christian women's magazine, this is her first book. While attending a huge women's conference, she was overcome by the leading of the Holy Spirit to write her story and the stories of others. While standing and singing a worship song, she felt compelled to retrieve her pen and paper as titles for these ten chapters on grief came to her mind. She began to interview other widows and their friends and relatives. Along with her own stories, she organized these into the appropriate chapters. She has used her story telling skills to reel in readers as they make connections and receive help in their own journeys.

Her personal testimony is one of overcoming family issues such as being reared by her widowed high-functioning alcoholic mother. Even though her mother did not attend church, she sent all six of her children. There, Paula saw and heard about the grace and love of Jesus. She accepted Christ as her savior at the age of twelve. A year later, while attending church camp, she made a complete surrender to him and felt a call into full time ministry. She reports that God's calling and continuing direction have held her steady and enthusiastic through the years with challenges of

- caring for aging parents,
- moving seven times to different pastorates,
- teaching in public schools,
- loving and ministering to a prodigal son,
- losing the love of her life,
- living and thriving as a single person.

She testifies that God's grace has always been and will continue to be sufficient. His strength is surely made perfect in her weakness (2 Cor. 12:9).